THE
GEMAYELS

THE GEMAYELS

Matthew S. Gordon

CHELSEA HOUSE PUBLISHERS
NEW YORK
PHILADELPHIA

EDITOR-IN-CHIEF: Nancy Toff
EXECUTIVE EDITOR: Remmel T. Nunn
MANAGING EDITOR: Karyn Gullen Browne
COPY CHIEF: Juliann Barbato
PICTURE EDITOR: Adrian G. Allen
ART DIRECTOR: Giannella Garrett
MANUFACTURING MANAGER: Gerald Levine

Staff for THE GEMAYELS:

SENIOR EDITOR: John W. Selfridge
COPY EDITOR: Karen Hammonds
DEPUTY COPY CHIEF: Ellen Scordato
EDITORIAL ASSISTANT: Sean Ginty
ASSOCIATE PICTURE EDITOR: Juliette Dickstein
PICTURE RESEARCHER: Elie Porter
DESIGNER: Jill Goldreyer
PRODUCTION COORDINATOR: Joseph Romano
COVER ILLUSTRATION: David Dircks

3 5 7 9 8 6 4 2

Library of Congress Cataloging in Publication Data

Gordon, Matthew S.
    The Gemayels.

    (World leaders past & present)
    Bibliography: p.
    Includes index.
    Summary: Examines the life of the current president of Lebanon and
that of his predecessor, who was his brother.

1. Jumayyil, Bashīr, 1947–1982—Juvenile literature.
2. Jumayyil, Amīn—Juvenile literature. 3. Lebanon—
Presidents—Biography—Juvenile literature.
[1. Jumayyil, Bashīr, 1947–1982. 2. Jumayyil, Amīn.
3. Lebanon—Presidents] I. Title. II. Series.
DS87.2.A2G67   1988   956.92′044′0924 [920]   87-33756
ISBN 1-55546-834-9
      0-7910-0570-4 (pbk.)

Contents

JOHN ADAMS
JOHN QUINCY ADAMS
KONRAD ADENAUER
ALEXANDER THE GREAT
SALVADOR ALLENDE
MARC ANTONY
CORAZON AQUINO
YASIR ARAFAT
KING ARTHUR
HAFEZ AL-ASSAD
KEMAL ATATÜRK
ATTILA
CLEMENT ATTLEE
AUGUSTUS CAESAR
MENACHEM BEGIN
DAVID BEN-GURION
OTTO VON BISMARCK
LÉON BLUM
SIMON BOLÍVAR
CESARE BORGIA
WILLY BRANDT
LEONID BREZHNEV
JULIUS CAESAR
JOHN CALVIN
JIMMY CARTER
FIDEL CASTRO
CATHERINE THE GREAT
CHARLEMAGNE
CHIANG KAI-SHEK
WINSTON CHURCHILL
GEORGES CLEMENCEAU
CLEOPATRA
CONSTANTINE THE GREAT
HERNÁN CORTÉS
OLIVER CROMWELL
GEORGES-JACQUES
   DANTON
JEFFERSON DAVIS
MOSHE DAYAN
CHARLES DE GAULLE
EAMON DE VALERA
EUGENE DEBS
DENG XIAOPING
BENJAMIN DISRAELI
ALEXANDER DUBČEK
FRANÇOIS & JEAN-CLAUDE
   DUVALIER
DWIGHT EISENHOWER
ELEANOR OF AQUITAINE
ELIZABETH I
FAISAL
FERDINAND & ISABELLA
FRANCISCO FRANCO
BENJAMIN FRANKLIN

FREDERICK THE GREAT
INDIRA GANDHI
MOHANDAS GANDHI
GIUSEPPE GARIBALDI
AMIN & BASHIR GEMAYEL
GENGHIS KHAN
WILLIAM GLADSTONE
MIKHAIL GORBACHEV
ULYSSES S. GRANT
ERNESTO "CHE" GUEVARA
TENZIN GYATSO
ALEXANDER HAMILTON
DAG HAMMARSKJÖLD
HENRY VIII
HENRY OF NAVARRE
PAUL VON HINDENBURG
HIROHITO
ADOLF HITLER
HO CHI MINH
KING HUSSEIN
IVAN THE TERRIBLE
ANDREW JACKSON
JAMES I
WOJCIECH JARUZELSKI
THOMAS JEFFERSON
JOAN OF ARC
POPE JOHN XXIII
POPE JOHN PAUL II
LYNDON JOHNSON
BENITO JUÁREZ
JOHN KENNEDY
ROBERT KENNEDY
JOMO KENYATTA
AYATOLLAH KHOMEINI
NIKITA KHRUSHCHEV
KIM IL SUNG
MARTIN LUTHER KING, JR.
HENRY KISSINGER
KUBLAI KHAN
LAFAYETTE
ROBERT E. LEE
VLADIMIR LENIN
ABRAHAM LINCOLN
DAVID LLOYD GEORGE
LOUIS XIV
MARTIN LUTHER
JUDAS MACCABEUS
JAMES MADISON
NELSON & WINNIE
   MANDELA
MAO ZEDONG
FERDINAND MARCOS
GEORGE MARSHALL

MARY, QUEEN OF SCOTS
TOMÁŠ MASARYK
GOLDA MEIR
KLEMENS VON METTERNICH
JAMES MONROE
HOSNI MUBARAK
ROBERT MUGABE
BENITO MUSSOLINI
NAPOLÉON BONAPARTE
GAMAL ABDEL NASSER
JAWAHARLAL NEHRU
NERO
NICHOLAS II
RICHARD NIXON
KWAME NKRUMAH
DANIEL ORTEGA
MOHAMMED REZA PAHLAVI
THOMAS PAINE
CHARLES STEWART
   PARNELL
PERICLES
JUAN PERÓN
PETER THE GREAT
POL POT
MUAMMAR EL-QADDAFI
RONALD REAGAN
CARDINAL RICHELIEU
MAXIMILIEN ROBESPIERRE
ELEANOR ROOSEVELT
FRANKLIN ROOSEVELT
THEODORE ROOSEVELT
ANWAR SADAT
HAILE SELASSIE
PRINCE SIHANOUK
JAN SMUTS
JOSEPH STALIN
SUKARNO
SUN YAT-SEN
TAMERLANE
MOTHER TERESA
MARGARET THATCHER
JOSIP BROZ TITO
TOUSSAINT L'OUVERTURE
LEON TROTSKY
PIERRE TRUDEAU
HARRY TRUMAN
QUEEN VICTORIA
LECH WALESA
GEORGE WASHINGTON
CHAIM WEIZMANN
WOODROW WILSON
XERXES
EMILIANO ZAPATA
ZHOU ENLAI

CHELSEA HOUSE PUBLISHERS

ON LEADERSHIP

Arthur M. Schlesinger, jr.

LEADERSHIP, it may be said, is really what makes the world go round. Love no doubt smooths the passage; but love is a private transaction between consenting adults. Leadership is a public trans-action with history. The idea of leadership affirms the capacity of individuals to move, inspire, and mobilize masses of people so that they act together in pursuit of an end. Sometimes leadership serves good purposes, sometimes bad; but whether the end is benign or evil, great leaders are those men and women who leave their personal stamp on history.

Now, the very concept of leadership implies the proposition that individuals can make a difference. This proposition has never been universally accepted. From classical times to the present day, eminent thinkers have regarded individuals as no more than the agents and pawns of larger forces, whether the gods and goddesses of the ancient world or, in the modern era, race, class, nation, the dialectic, the will of the people, the spirit of the times, history itself. Against such forces, the individual dwindles into insignificance.

So contends the thesis of historical determinism. Tolstoy's great novel *War and Peace* offers a famous statement of the case. Why, Tolstoy asked, did millions of men in the Napoleonic Wars, denying their human feelings and their common sense, move back and forth across Europe slaughtering their fellows? "The war," Tolstoy answered, "was bound to happen simply because it was bound to happen." All prior history predetermined it. As for leaders, they, Tolstoy said, "are but the labels that serve to give a name to an end and, like labels, they have the least possible connection with the event." The greater the leader, "the more conspicuous the inev-itability and the predestination of every act he commits." The leader, said Tolstoy, is "the slave of history."

Determinism takes many forms. Marxism is the determinism of class. Nazism the determinism of race. But the idea of men and women as the slaves of history runs athwart the deepest human instincts. Rigid determinism abolishes the idea of human freedom—

the assumption of free choice that underlies every move we make, every word we speak, every thought we think. It abolishes the idea of human responsibility, since it is manifestly unfair to reward or punish people for actions that are by definition beyond their control. No one can live consistently by any deterministic creed. The Marxist states prove this themselves by their extreme susceptibility to the cult of leadership.

More than that, history refutes the idea that individuals make no difference. In December 1931 a British politician crossing Park Avenue in New York City between 76th and 77th Streets around 10:30 P.M. looked in the wrong direction and was knocked down by an automobile—a moment, he later recalled, of a man aghast, a world aglare: "I do not understand why I was not broken like an eggshell or squashed like a gooseberry." Fourteen months later an American politician, sitting in an open car in Miami, Florida, was fired on by an assassin; the man beside him was hit. Those who believe that individuals make no difference to history might well ponder whether the next two decades would have been the same had Mario Constasino's car killed Winston Churchill in 1931 and Giuseppe Zangara's bullet killed Franklin Roosevelt in 1933. Suppose, in addition, that Adolf Hitler had been killed in the street fighting during the Munich *Putsch* of 1923 and that Lenin had died of typhus during World War I. What would the 20th century be like now?

For better or for worse, individuals do make a difference. "The notion that a people can run itself and its affairs anonymously," wrote the philosopher William James, "is now well known to be the silliest of absurdities. Mankind does nothing save through initiatives on the part of inventors, great or small, and imitation by the rest of us—these are the sole factors in human progress. Individuals of genius show the way, and set the patterns, which common people then adopt and follow."

Leadership, James suggests, means leadership in thought as well as in action. In the long run, leaders in thought may well make the greater difference to the world. But, as Woodrow Wilson once said, "Those only are leaders of men, in the general eye, who lead in action. . . . It is at their hands that new thought gets its translation into the crude language of deeds." Leaders in thought often invent in solitude and obscurity, leaving to later generations the tasks of imitation. Leaders in action—the leaders portrayed in this series—have to be effective in their own time.

And they cannot be effective by themselves. They must act in response to the rhythms of their age. Their genius must be adapted, in a phrase of William James's, "to the receptivities of the moment." Leaders are useless without followers. "There goes the mob," said the French politician hearing a clamor in the streets. "I am their leader. I must follow them." Great leaders turn the inchoate emotions of the mob to purposes of their own. They seize on the opportunities of their time, the hopes, fears, frustrations, crises, potentialities. They succeed when events have prepared the way for them, when the community is awaiting to be aroused, when they can provide the clarifying and organizing ideas. Leadership ignites the circuit between the individual and the mass and thereby alters history.

It may alter history for better or for worse. Leaders have been responsible for the most extravagant follies and most monstrous crimes that have beset suffering humanity. They have also been vital in such gains as humanity has made in individual freedom, religious and racial tolerance, social justice, and respect for human rights.

There is no sure way to tell in advance who is going to lead for good and who for evil. But a glance at the gallery of men and women in *World Leaders—Past and Present* suggests some useful tests.

One test is this: Do leaders lead by force or by persuasion? By command or by consent? Through most of history leadership was exercised by the divine right of authority. The duty of followers was to defer and to obey. "Theirs not to reason why / Theirs but to do and die." On occasion, as with the so-called enlightened despots of the 18th century in Europe, absolutist leadership was animated by humane purposes. More often, absolutism nourished the passion for domination, land, gold, and conquest and resulted in tyranny.

The great revolution of modern times has been the revolution of equality. The idea that all people should be equal in their legal condition has undermined the old structure of authority, hierarchy, and deference. The revolution of equality has had two contrary effects on the nature of leadership. For equality, as Alexis de Tocqueville pointed out in his great study *Democracy in America*, might mean equality in servitude as well as equality in freedom.

"I know of only two methods of establishing equality in the political world," Tocqueville wrote. "Rights must be given to every citizen, or none at all to anyone . . . save one, who is the master of all." There was no middle ground "between the sovereignty of all and the absolute power of one man." In his astonishing prediction of 20th-century totalitarian dictatorship, Tocqueville explained how the revolution of equality could lead to the *"Führerprinzip"* and more terrible absolutism than the world had ever known.

But when rights are given to every citizen and the sovereignty of all is established, the problem of leadership takes a new form, becomes more exacting than ever before. It is easy to issue commands and enforce them by the rope and the stake, the concentration camp and the *gulag.* It is much harder to use argument and achievement to overcome opposition and win consent. The Founding Fathers of the United States understood the difficulty. They believed that history had given them the opportunity to decide, as Alexander Hamilton wrote in the first Federalist Paper, whether men are indeed capable of basing government on "reflection and choice, or whether they are forever destined to depend . . . on accident and force."

Government by reflection and choice called for a new style of leadership and a new quality of followership. It required leaders to be responsive to popular concerns, and it required followers to be active and informed participants in the process. Democracy does not eliminate emotion from politics; sometimes it fosters demagoguery; but it is confident that, as the greatest of democratic leaders put it, you cannot fool all of the people all of the time. It measures leadership by results and retires those who overreach or falter or fail.

It is true that in the long run despots are measured by results too. But they can postpone the day of judgment, sometimes indefinitely, and in the meantime they can do infinite harm. It is also true that democracy is no guarantee of virtue and intelligence in government, for the voice of the people is not necessarily the voice of God. But democracy, by assuring the right of opposition, offers built-in resistance to the evils inherent in absolutism. As the theologian Reinhold Niebuhr summed it up, "Man's capacity for justice makes democracy possible, but man's inclination to injustice makes democracy necessary."

A second test for leadership is the end for which power is sought. When leaders have as their goal the supremacy of a master race or the promotion of totalitarian revolution or the acquisition and exploitation of colonies or the protection of greed and privilege or the preservation of personal power, it is likely that their leadership will do little to advance the cause of humanity. When their goal is the abolition of slavery, the liberation of women, the enlargement of opportunity for the poor and powerless, the extension of equal rights to racial minorities, the defense of the freedoms of expression and opposition, it is likely that their leadership will increase the sum of human liberty and welfare.

Leaders have done great harm to the world. They have also conferred great benefits. You will find both sorts in this series. Even "good" leaders must be regarded with a certain wariness. Leaders are not demigods; they put on their trousers one leg after another just like ordinary mortals. No leader is infallible, and every leader needs to be reminded of this at regular intervals. Irreverence irritates leaders but is their salvation. Unquestioning submission corrupts leaders and demeans followers. Making a cult of a leader is always a mistake. Fortunately hero worship generates its own antidote. "Every hero," said Emerson, "becomes a bore at last."

The signal benefit the great leaders confer is to embolden the rest of us to live according to our own best selves, to be active, insistent, and resolute in affirming our own sense of things. For great leaders attest to the reality of human freedom against the supposed inevitabilities of history. And they attest to the wisdom and power that may lie within the most unlikely of us, which is why Abraham Lincoln remains the supreme example of great leadership. A great leader, said Emerson, exhibits new possibilities to all humanity. "We feed on genius. . . . Great men exist that there may be greater men."

Great leaders, in short, justify themselves by emancipating and empowering their followers. So humanity struggles to master its destiny, remembering with Alexis de Tocqueville: "It is true that around every man a fatal circle is traced beyond which he cannot pass; but within the wide verge of that circle he is powerful and free; as it is with man, so with communities."

1

A Country in Crisis

Situated at the eastern end of the Mediterranean Sea and bordered by Israel and Syria, modern Lebanon is a small country whose population comprises a large number of separate religious communities. During the 1970s it was one of the Middle East's most prosperous and dynamic states. In 1975, however, Lebanon entered a period of turmoil and bloodshed. Political and economic collapse soon followed.

By September 1982, a variety of armed groups — including the Syrian army, the Israeli Defense Forces (IDF), and a variety of Lebanese sectarian militias — dominated the entire country. The Lebanese economy, still relatively strong despite the deteriorating political situation, had experienced severe inflation and fluctuations in the value of the currency. Loss of life and destruction of property had been extensive. Aggravating the situation was that the social, political, and religious differences that had driven Lebanon's numerous communities into conflict were growing only greater.

On September 14, 1982, the problems facing the people of Lebanon took yet another turn for the worse. At 4:10 P.M., in the eastern section of Beirut, the Lebanese capital, a bomb devastated the headquarters of the Kataib party, the strongest of Leb-

Lebanon was never meant to be—nor shall it be—a theatre for terrorism and violence; but rather an impregnable fortress of security and peace, of justice and democracy.
—AMIN GEMAYEL

Amin Gemayel, newly elected president of Lebanon, addresses the Lebanese parliament on September 21, 1982. Hanging above him is a picture of his brother, Bashir Gemayel, who was elected to the same office only a month earlier but was assassinated on September 14.

Bashir Gemayel inspects a group of his armed followers, the Maronite Christian militia, known as the Lebanese Forces. Deeply loyal to Bashir, this militia achieved dominance over the Christian community in Lebanon through a series of attacks against other Christian militias.

anon's Christian political parties. The blast turned much of the three-story building into a heap of shattered concrete and twisted metal. During the next few hours, party members, neighborhood residents, and emergency service personnel worked furiously to extricate the dead and wounded. Among the victims was the newly elected president of Lebanon, 34-year-old Bashir Gemayel.

Shortly after 10:00 P.M. rescue workers found Gemayel. The president, who had suffered terrible injuries to his head and back, was immediately rushed to the nearby Hotel Dieu Hospital, where the doctors pronounced him dead. The difficult task of formally announcing Gemayel's death was given to Karim Pakradouni, an intellectual and top aide to the Gemayel family. Pakradouni returned to party headquarters and quietly told Gemayel's followers what they most dreaded hearing. Their fury and despair would soon find expression in a new cycle of killing and destruction.

It was by no means immediately apparent who was responsible for the bombing, which killed 8 party members and injured more than 50. There were many groups, both at home and abroad, that had had good reason to hate Gemayel. Most of them had refused to support his election as president, and few would have hesitated to use violence against him. After extensive investigations by both the Kataib party and the Lebanese government, a suspect named Habib Shartuni was arrested. Shartuni was known to have worked for Syrian intelligence. His family belonged to the Syrian Socialist Nationalist party (SSNP), a pro-Syrian Lebanese party with a long history of opposition to the Kataib. Shartuni eventually confessed to having planted the bomb; however, it remains unclear to this day who actually planned the operation.

Six days after Gemayel's death, the deputies of the Lebanese Parliament gathered to elect a new president. By an overwhelming majority they chose Amin Gemayel, Bashir's elder brother. In his inaugural address, Amin spoke of his brother as a martyr and of the importance of honoring his mem-

Bashir Gemayel was the youngest child of Pierre and Genevieve Gemayel. Like his father and older brother, Amin, Bashir became involved in Lebanese politics as a teenager.

Karim Pakradouni, a Maronite Christian, was a member of the politburo of the Kataib party, the political organization founded by Pierre Gemayel in 1936. Pakradouni went on to become a close adviser to Bashir Gemayel in the 1970s.

ory. He also vowed to do his utmost to realize Bashir's dreams for Lebanon's future.

Amin and his brother were quite unalike in both temperament and in their political views. These differences had often caused tensions between the two. After Bashir's assassination, Amin had trouble winning support from Bashir's followers in the Christian community and the Kataib. This led to serious divisions within the community that, in turn, helped complicate the country's political situation.

Bashir was shorter and stockier than Amin. Unlike Amin, known for his urbane appearance, Bashir was comfortable in casual dress and, as a military commander, often wore a fatigue jacket. Bashir was the more energetic and even fiery of the two. Amin is more poised and calmer in manner. Whereas Bashir had the reputation of making quick, even rash, decisions, Amin is more deliberate in his choices, to the point of being accused by his enemies of being indecisive.

In the political sphere, Amin is known as a moderate. Having spent much of his adult life as a member of the Lebanese Parliament, he has shown a willingness to compromise and, on occasion, an ability to cooperate even with those whose views differ from his own. More importantly, however, Amin has not displayed the charisma of his younger brother. During his career, Bashir managed to secure a large and loyal following whose members accorded him their personal allegiance. Amin, when he became president, had a smaller following, and one whose loyalty to him was much less intense than that of followers of Bashir. After his brother's death, Amin would encounter serious problems in dealing with Bashir's supporters. Those, however, were not the only difficulties he would face.

The man accused of setting the explosion that killed Bashir Gemayel, Habib Shartuni, sits between two members of the Lebanese Forces. It remains unclear to the present day who actually planned the assassination.

Amin Gemayel (center) and members of the Kataib and the Lebanese Forces follow Bashir's coffin. Bashir was buried in the mountain village of Bikfayah, the home of the Gemayel family for many generations.

Amin Gemayel was elected to the presidency of a country that was deeply divided. Over the previous seven years it had become little more than a shadow of a nation, riven by civil strife and tormented still further by the armed intervention of foreign powers. As the weak and deeply troubled neighbor of Syria and Israel, Lebanon not only was torn by internal struggles but also was a victim of the larger Arab-Israeli dispute. This conflict between the Jewish state and its Arab neighbors had dominated Middle Eastern politics over the past 40 years. As the fighting in Lebanon grew worse after 1975, the government in Beirut steadily decreased in power. The leaders of Israel, Syria and other nations showed few qualms about using the Lebanese crisis for their own gain. Through large sums of money, arms shipments and political pressures, these outside countries encouraged the Lebanese to keep killing one another. Lebanon thus became the arena in which these countries could fight out their political and military battles. The internal crisis in Lebanon became much harder to solve as a result.

Before one can understand Lebanon's position — and Amin Gemayel's predicament — within this broader context, some understanding of the history of Lebanon itself is essential.

At the beginning of the 20th century, Lebanon was smaller than it is today. At that time, it comprised only the mountain range known as Mount Lebanon. It did not yet include Beirut, the Beqa Valley, or the cities of Sidon and Tripoli and their environs. Mount Lebanon was inhabited by several different religious communities. These included the Maronite Christians, Catholics who recognize the authority of the pope but practice their own rites; and the Druze, a distinct sect with historical roots in Shi'a Islam, the smaller of Islam's two main branches. (The larger, so-called orthodox Islamic grouping is known as Sunni Islam; its adherents are referred to as Sunnis.) Technically, Mount Lebanon constituted part of the Ottoman Turkish Empire. However, the power of the empire had declined substantially during the previous two centuries, and the various communities of Mount Lebanon enjoyed considerable autonomy.

The Maronite community in Mount Lebanon has a long history. It is believed that in the 8th century the Maronites fled from religious persecution in Syria and settled in Mount Lebanon. There they built churches and villages and, until the 16th century, lived mainly as peasants. In the 16th and 17th centuries, however, the Maronites' role began to change. During this period, powerful Druze families serving as local governors for the Ottoman Turks controlled Mount Lebanon. It was under the Druze that the Maronites began to increase their political power. It was also during the 17th century that Westerners first established a presence in Lebanon. Catholic missionaries set up schools in Maronite areas, and the resulting increase in the level of education among the Maronites contributed to the rise in the social and political status of the sect.

During the 18th and 19th centuries, the Maronite

As early as the eighteenth century, foreign travelers remarked upon the atmosphere of liberty in Lebanon, and rightly so. It was partly this liberty that made the Lebanon of yesterday so compelling, but in so fragmented a society, it also constituted a danger to the nation's cohesion.
—DAVID C. GORDON
American historian

A line of armored personnel carriers of the Lebanese Army moves through the Christian sector of Beirut, the Lebanese capital. Above them is a picture of Bashir Gemayel; the caption, in Arabic, reads "You are our president for all time."

community gradually attained political dominance in Lebanon. The Maronite peasantry and middle classes, supported by the Maronite church, began to challenge the power of the Maronite and Druze *zu'ama*, or traditional leaders. These men exercised control in their respective areas through a combination of personal authority and armed force. Their say on social, political, and economic questions was usually final. (Each *za'im*, as individual traditional leaders were known, was expected to protect the political and economic interests of the people of the region he controlled. His followers, who were usually of the same religious group as the za'im, would accord him their support and, in time of crisis, bear arms to defend both the za'im and his domain. This attachment of a local community to the leading family of a region remains an important aspect of Lebanese politics to this day.)

In the summer of 1860, tensions between the Maronites and the Druze finally erupted into open warfare. The Druze, who have long enjoyed a reputation for military prowess, gained the upper hand in the fighting, inflicting considerable casualties on the Maronites at little cost to themselves. At this point France, with the active support of several other Eu-

Prior to the 20th century, Lebanon comprised only the rugged mountain range now called Mount Lebanon. In 1920, under the rule of the French, Beirut and other areas were annexed to the Mount to create Greater Lebanon.

ropean powers, intervened on the side of the Maronites. They pressured the Ottoman Turks to establish a new administrative system for Mount Lebanon.

Under the new system, which was known as the Special Regime and whose terms were dictated by the European powers, the privileges of the ruling families were abolished. Salaried officials of the Ottoman government became responsible for tax collection, and district and village taxes were assessed by a new body known as the Administrative Council. This body comprised 12 members representing the 6 sects that then inhabited Mount Lebanon. The council contained four Maronites, three Druze, two Greek Orthodox members, one Greek Catholic, one Sunni, and one Shi'i.

Although the imposition of the new administrative system brought an end to the bloodshed, the Maronites would nurse the memory of the disaster that had befallen them for many years to come. Memories of 1860 fueled their distrust of other groups and helped convince their community that it would always have to be prepared to defend itself.

As relations between Mount Lebanon and the West developed, Mount Lebanon emerged as a strong mercantile power in the trade between the West and the rest of the Middle East. Slowly, as a result of this interaction, western social and political ideas came to influence many Lebanese. This exposure to new ways of thinking was accompanied by exposure to new types of technology as westerners introduced such things as printing presses, railways, and modern firearms.

Reaction to western penetration in Mount Lebanon differed from community to community. The Christians, and especially the Maronites, were involved early on in trade with the West, and they had derived greater benefits from the newly established schools than the Druze and the Muslim communities. They also shared the same religious beliefs as the Europeans. As a result, many Maronites began to identify with western attitudes and institutions.

The response of their Muslim neighbors was quite different. Many Muslims were critical of western ideas and technology. They considered the values taught in the new schools incompatible with those of Islam and viewed the schools themselves as a challenge to traditional Muslim education. Some Lebanese Muslims condemned the political and commercial activities of the western powers as demonstrating nothing but a selfish desire to take advantage of Lebanon's relative political and economic weakness.

By the beginning of the 20th century, the Maronite community had developed a strong identity. Some Maronite intellectuals began to speak of their

Elders of the Druze faith are the traditional spokesmen of their community. The Druze, like the Maronite Christians, have inhabited Mount Lebanon for centuries. A large Druze population is also present in Israel.

community as a separate ethnic group with its own religious and historical background. They began to portray Mount Lebanon as having a unique history in which Maronites played the dominant role. In their view, Mount Lebanon was essentially a special Maronite homeland, a territory in which Maronites were the largest single group. There were also some Maronites who claimed that Mount Lebanon was different from the rest of the Middle East, that it was not really an Arab region. Increasingly, these thinkers looked not to the Arab world but to the West, especially to France.

Following the end of the conflict between the Maronites and the Druze, Mount Lebanon remained at peace until November 1915, when Turkey entered World War I, siding with Germany and Austria-Hungary against Great Britain and France. In defiance of the treaties that had established the Special Regime, the Ottoman Turkish government sent troops into Mount Lebanon to occupy the country. For the next three years, until 1918, when the war ended with Germany's defeat, the people of Mount Lebanon suffered terrible food shortages and widespread repression as the Turks stripped the area of resources to support their war effort. In 1920, under the terms of a mandate granted by the League of Nations, France became the governing power in Lebanon. In September of that same year, the French high commissioner proclaimed the creation of Greater Lebanon, which comprised Mount Lebanon, the Beqa Valley, Tripoli, Beirut, Sidon, the port city of Tyre, and the southern regions of Rashaya and Hasbaya, which were annexed from Syria.

During the period of the French Mandate, Lebanon underwent several important social and political changes that had profound implications for the country's future. In 1926, a Lebanese republic was established under French auspices, with a constitution written by a Maronite, Michel Chiha. The constitution stated that Lebanon would be governed by a president and a single parliament. It also attempted to settle the all-important issue of how best to distribute political power among the country's communities.

My Lebanon, which I drew at times so close around me, was a cloak of many colors. Beirut was Levantine to the heart, astute, multilingual, many-minded and within an element of sheer bawdy wickedness.
—ALBION ROSS
American author, on pre–Civil War Lebanon

By attaching Beirut and other areas to Mount Lebanon, the French had brought together a wide variety of disparate communities: the Maronites in Mount Lebanon and the south; the Greek Orthodox Christians in Lebanon's northern areas; the Druze; the Sunnis, many of whom lived in the northern Akkar region as well as in Beirut and other urban centers; and the Shi'is, who lived mainly in the Beqa Valley and the Jabal 'Amil area, which lies to the south of Sidon. To solve the problem of representation, it was decided to distribute both government posts and parliamentary seats according to the size of each sect. A census taken in 1932 determined that the Maronites made up the largest community, followed by the Sunnis and the Shi'is. On this basis, parliamentary seats were distributed in the ratio of five Muslim seats for every six Christian seats. It was also agreed that the president of the new state would be a Maronite, the prime minister a Sunni, and the speaker of the Parliament a Shi'i.

Most Maronites had welcomed the creation of Greater Lebanon, believing that under the French they could build a state in which they would enjoy predominance. The Sunnis, however, took a different view of the situation. Under the Ottoman Turks, who were also Sunnis, the Lebanese Sunnis had enjoyed certain political and commercial privileges.

Before the outbreak of civil war in 1975, Beirut was one of the most dynamic and cosmopolitan cities of the eastern Mediterranean. Even into the 1980s, after years of violence and destruction, the Lebanese capital remained a financial and intellectual center for the entire Middle East.

With their incorporation into Greater Lebanon, the Sunnis of Sidon, Tripoli, and Beirut suddenly found themselves a minority in the new state. They were forced to accept the political domination of the non-Muslim, French-backed Maronites. Opposition to the Maronite ascendancy was also widespread among the Greek Orthodox Christians, the Druze, and the Shi'is. During the 1920s and 1930s, it became increasingly apparent that the greatest problem facing Lebanon was the political consequences of its social fragmentation. Many Lebanese were torn between two loyalties, one to their community, the other to the state. Finding a way of preventing the tensions resulting from this fragmentation from turning into outright warfare became the greatest challenge facing the country's leaders.

In 1941, two years after the outbreak of World War II and one year after France had fallen to the Germans, Lebanon was occupied by Free French forces. The Free French, led by General Charles de Gaulle, were bitterly opposed to the collaborationist government in Paris. The French commander in Lebanon, General Georges Catroux, ousted the collaborationist administration in Lebanon and assumed responsibility for governing the country. In 1943, under pressure from Great Britain and the United States, which had entered the war on Great Britain's side in December 1941, de Gaulle agreed to transfer all remaining political powers to the Lebanese on January 1, 1944. The question of political representation in the new government remained hotly contended, however, and remains so to this day. Lebanon's problems have only multiplied in the years since 1944.

2

The Creation of a Dynasty

Amin Gemayel was born on January 22, 1942, in Bikfayah, a small mountain village in the region of Lebanon known as the Metn, which is situated to the north of Beirut. He was the first child of Pierre Gemayel, an influential Christian politician and the leader of the Kataib party, and Genevieve Gemayel. Bikfayah has been the home of the Gemayel family for centuries.

Amin, like many Lebanese Christian children, received both his elementary and his secondary education at schools run by Catholic religious orders. He attended the Collège Notre Dame de Jamhour, a private Catholic institution. Lessons at the school were conducted entirely in French. However, Amin probably spoke both French and Arabic at home. Like most children of his class and background, he became fluent in both languages. Following his graduation from the Collège Notre Dame de Jamhour, Amin enrolled in the School of Law at Beirut's Université de St. Joseph. A privately funded institution, the Université de St. Joseph is one of Lebanon's top universities. In 1965, Amin graduated from law school and began working as an attorney in Beirut.

The monument which characterizes the ethos of Lebanon is to be found north along the Mediterranean. It is the government operated Casino du Liban, where dollars change hands on a throw of the dice or a turn of the wheel.
—JOSEPH MALONE
author

Bashir and Amin Gemayel, with their wives Solange and Joyce and their parents Pierre and Genevieve. The Gemayels were not one of the traditional leading families of the Christian Maronite community. It was only through Pierre's aggressive leadership that the family became a leading Maronite clan.

In the 1950s, the Martyrs Square area was an important commercial district in Lebanon's rapidly growing young capital, Beirut. In 1916, the governor of the Ottoman Empire, which then encompassed much of the Middle East, had a group of Lebanese nationalists put to death. The square was named in their memory.

By this time, however, Pierre Gemayel had come to consider Amin a suitable successor not only to the position of head of the Gemayel family but to the leadership of the Kataib party. It was on the urging of his father that Amin began his political career.

Born in 1905, Pierre Gemayel was the son of Sheikh Amin Gemayel, a wealthy doctor with a reputation as an ardent Francophile and a bitter opponent of the Ottoman Turks. During World War I, Sheikh Amin's criticisms of the Turks led to his expulsion from Mount Lebanon by the Turkish authorities. The Gemayel family spent the war years in exile in Egypt, which was then a British protectorate. After the war, the family returned to Mount Lebanon, where Pierre completed his education, eventually graduating from the Université de St. Joseph with a degree in pharmacy. For a brief period in the early 1930s, Pierre worked as a pharmacist at a hospital in Paris. After his return to Mount Lebanon, he took over a pharmacy owned by the Gemayel family in downtown Beirut's Martyrs Square.

Throughout this period, Pierre Gemayel remained a sports enthusiast. A tall and muscular young man, he boxed, wrestled, and played soccer with all the passion and intensity that he would later bring to politics.

In 1936, at age 21, Pierre Gemayel was chosen to play on Lebanon's Olympic soccer team. The Olympic Games were held that year in the German capital, Berlin. At that time Germany was ruled by the fascist National Socialist German Workers' party (NSDAP), which is more commonly known as the Nazi party. Adolf Hitler, Germany's violently anti-communist and profoundly anti-Semitic leader, hoped to use the games to showcase German fascism. He wanted to demonstrate to the world that Germany had become an orderly and disciplined country during the three years since the Nazis' accession to power. Though most observers found the regimentation and uniformity that Nazism had forced upon German society thoroughly disturbing, others found the new Germany highly impressive. Pierre Gemayel, who fell into the latter category, was moved to write: "We orientals are by nature an unruly and individualistic people. In Germany I witnessed the perfect conduct of a whole unified nation."

Adolf Hitler, the dictator of Nazi Germany, presided over the 1936 Olympic Games, which were held in Berlin. Pierre Gemayel, then a member of the Lebanese Olympic soccer team, later said that the Nazi movement helped inspire him to create the Kataib party.

Young men in Czechoslovakia receive military training prior to World War II. Pierre Gemayel visited Czechoslovakia in 1936, as a member of the Lebanese Olympic soccer team; he was impressed by the activities of the Czech Sokol movement, a paramilitary group.

Also in 1936 Pierre Gemayel visited Czechoslovakia, a Central European state that was then one of the world's most advanced democracies. There he observed the activities of the Sokols, a paramilitary youth organization. Pierre returned to Lebanon in November 1936, and he and five other Maronites, inspired by the new right-wing mass movements developing in Europe, decided to found a new political movement of their own. They called their organization al-Kataib al-Lubnaniya, or Lebanese Falange, commonly called the Kataib. Pierre had borrowed the name from the Spanish right-wing paramilitary movement known as the Falange, which later became the Traditionalist Spanish Falange, the political party that served Spain's fascist dictator, General Francisco Franco. The motto of the Kataib was "God, Fatherland, and Country." (The Kataib is frequently referred to by its French name, the Phalanges Libanaises.) Pierre Gemayel's

French general Henri Gouraud (left) parades with his troops in Beirut in 1920. Gouraud became the first French High Commissioner in Beirut when the French gained control of Syria and Lebanon after World War I.

colleagues named him *chef supérieur*, or president, of the organization. As historian and journalist Tabitha Petran notes in *The Struggle over Lebanon*, the Kataib was "authoritarian, its leader all powerful; the emphasis was on obedience, unquestioning discipline, and military training. Its members paraded in uniform and gave the fascist salute."

Pierre Gemayel was a natural leader. Energetic and dedicated, he seemed to thrive on hard work and demanded a great deal from his followers. Although he was neither very well read nor particularly thoughtful, he had immense drive and sincerity. He was also somewhat of a martinet. From 1936 on, he devoted all his energies to furthering the cause of the Kataib. At first he viewed the Kataib as an apolitical organization. In January 1937, he declared: "The [Kataib] does not constitute a political party. It is neither for nor against anyone; it is for Lebanon." Pierre Gemayel repeatedly asserted

Muslim and Christian Lebanese take part in a protest march in November 1943. After French officials arrested the Lebanese president, Bishara al-Khuri, and other members of the Lebanese government, protests became part of the nationalist movement in Lebanon.

that the goal of the movement was to build the bodies and minds of young Lebanese. Through training and discipline, he argued, his followers would help create a strong and modern Lebanon.

By 1938, the Kataib, which during the earliest phase of its existence resembled other paramilitary groups in the Middle East and Europe, would boast more than 8,000 members. And, as time passed, its leaders' claims that the organization was nonsectarian and purely nationalistic would be repeatedly challenged.

In 1937, Pierre Gemayel's concerns regarding Lebanon's political situation propelled the Kataib into political activity for the first time. Like many other Maronites, he felt strongly about the importance of defending the position and privileges of the Maronite community. As he saw it, the Maronites and Lebanon's other Christian communities were constantly threatened with domination by the Muslim majority beyond Lebanon's borders. His concerns in this respect had intensified early in 1936, when Muslim leaders from all over Lebanon staged a meeting in Beirut that they termed the "Conference of the Coast." The final statement issued by the conference called for the reintegration into Syria of all Muslim areas of Lebanon.

That members of the Syrian Popular party (PPS), the forerunner of the SSNP, attended the conference also disturbed Pierre Gemayel. The goal of the PPS, which had been founded by Antun Sa'dah, a member of Lebanon's Greek Orthodox community, in 1932, was to effect the unification of Lebanon and Syria and to secure independence for the new state. This was, of course, absolutely unacceptable to the Kataib and most Maronites.

Toward the middle of 1937, the good relations that the Kataib had enjoyed with the mandate government during the early months of the movement's existence began to sour. Gemayel and many other Kataib members had begun to identify themselves with the growing nationalist movement, which the French naturally considered a threat to their rule. In June, a rumor that the Tripoli region was to be annexed to Syria began to circulate. Gemayel responded to this development by announcing plans

Motorcycle patrols were among the forces used by the French colonial government to repress demonstrations against French rule in Lebanon in the early 1940s. Pierre Gemayel, the leader of the growing Kataib movement, was very active in these demonstrations.

Arab orphans cross the Lebanese-Israeli border in a 1949 agreement between the two countries to repatriate displaced children.

to call a general strike. The French, having failed to persuade Gemayel to retract his declaration, then issued a statement asserting that Lebanon's borders would not be redrawn. Gemayel accordingly called off the strike, but tensions between the Kataib and the French persisted.

On November 18, 1937, the French announced a ban on the Kataib and several other similar organizations and sent in troops to seize and close down their offices. On November 21 a large number of Kataib members and supporters, acting in defiance of an official ban on political gatherings, held a rally in Beirut to celebrate the first anniversary of the founding of the movement. When French troops intervened to disperse the demonstration, violence ensued. The soldiers opened fire, killing 2 members of the movement and wounding 70 others, including Pierre Gemayel. Along with many of his followers, he was then imprisoned.

News of the violence spread like wildfire, bringing thousands of ordinary Lebanese out into the streets in support of the jailed Kataib leaders. Faced with the threat of renewed violence, the French decided to release Gemayel and his colleagues. The Kataib had won a moral victory, and the prestige of the movement now began to rise.

The ban on the Kataib remained in place until 1943. The movement virtually ignored it, however. The Kataib continued to recruit new members and remained an active participant in the national struggle. In July 1938, the movement issued a statement in which it called itself "a purely Lebanese national institution" that was "fighting against all anti-nationalist doctrines which seek to destroy or diminish present-day Lebanon."

During World War II, Lebanon, like many other countries, faced severe economic problems. The mandate government's economic policies had always tended to benefit France rather than Lebanon itself, and in 1941 the Kataib decided to stage demonstrations to protest the totally inadequate system of food distribution that the French had established. A Sunni-led Muslim paramilitary group called the Najjada, which had been founded in 1937, joined the Kataib's protest campaign.

In November 1943, the Kataib and the Najjada organized a national strike, which the French im-

In May 1958, violence broke out in Lebanon that led to civil war. The 1958 crisis was instigated for the most part by the Lebanese president, Camille Chamoun, whose forceful efforts to quell the uprising deeply divided the Lebanese.

Demonstrators in Beirut contribute to the violence that swept over Lebanon in 1958. That crisis led to lasting divisions between the sectarian communities of Lebanon. Pierre Gemayel, although troubled by Chamoun's leadership, supported the government in the fighting.

mediately tried to crush by force. On November 13, Gemayel and many other protesters were arrested. The French released them a few days later, however. As a result of their activities Gemayel and the Kataib were now on their way to becoming important political players.

By the late 1940s, the Kataib had become identified with Pierre Gemayel and his family. Although the party had offices in many parts of Lebanon, it was strongest in those areas that had a majority Maronite population. Pierre himself, despite his original intentions, had begun to appear to his followers, and to act, as a za'im — the same type of traditional leader whose existence he had once considered a major impediment to Lebanon's evolution into a modern state. Like any other za'im, Pierre Gemayel now began to view the interests of his people as equal to, if not more important than, the interests of the nation as a whole.

The 1940s also witnessed a series of events in neighboring Palestine, then under British control. These events would have a profound effect on Lebanon's future. Shortly after World War II, the United Nations (UN), which replaced the League of Nations in 1945, proposed that Palestine be divided into two separate states, one for Arabs and one for Jews, with a small area in the southwest, known as the Gaza Strip, to be controlled by Egypt.

Many Jews within Palestine, backed by the Zionist movement, accepted this proposal. The Arab leadership hated the idea and continued to hope that one of the European powers would step in and block the creation of a new Jewish state. On May 15, 1948, two days after Israel formally achieved status as a nation, the armies of Egypt, Iraq, Lebanon, Syria, and Transjordan attacked.

Israel emerged victorious from the conflict, successfully defending its own borders and also winning territory that the UN had originally intended to be used for an Arab state in Palestine. Hundreds of thousands of Palestinian Arabs, fearing for their safety and terrified by the fighting, became refugees. Many of them fled to Lebanon. The majority of these were settled in refugee camps that eventually became strongholds of the Palestine Liberation Organization (PLO), a Palestinian Arab political and military umbrella organization that was founded in Jordan in 1964.

By the beginning of the 1960s, the Gemayels had emerged as one of Lebanon's most important leading families. At the same time, the Kataib had become a powerful and effective political and military movement. Shortly after Amin graduated from law school, Pierre Gemayel secured his son's election to the governing body of the Kataib, thus laying the foundations of Amin's political career.

In December 1970, Maurice Gemayel, Amin's uncle, died. Maurice had been a respected parliamentarian and a cabinet minister. After much debate within the Kataib's political bureau, and by a narrow vote of 13–12, Amin was nominated as the Kataib's candidate for the parliamentary seat that had fallen vacant with his uncle's death. Amin won the election and thus became, at age 28, a deputy in the Lebanese Parliament.

In 1972 national elections were held in Lebanon, and Amin was reelected to the same seat, which he would hold until his election to the presidency in 1982. In Parliament, Amin established himself as a

For more than forty years the erect and impressive figure of Pierre Gemayel has dominated the party he has led. During this long period he has persisted in his original purpose and mission but has been remarkably flexible in adapting the party to the changing circumstances.
—ITAMAR RABINOVICH
author

moderate. He developed useful contacts with many of his parliamentary colleagues and also became acquainted with leading members of the civil service and the Lebanese military. He frequently held discussions with the leaders of Lebanon's other sectarian communities. Later, as president, Amin would benefit from some of these contacts.

During the late 1960s and the 1970s, Amin Gemayel also pursued a wide range of activities outside the parliamentary arena. He showed considerable business acumen as an investor. He helped establish several professional associations and became the head of a number of athletic clubs. In 1977, Amin helped found *Panorama de l'Actualité*, a magazine that covered Lebanese and Middle Eastern affairs. In 1980 he began publishing *Le Reveil*, a French-language daily newspaper. He also played a key role in establishing a number of research institutions. During this same period, Amin developed a taste for traveling. He visited North America, several European countries, and a number of nations in the Middle East. In the Arab countries he visited, Amin frequently met with important political figures.

Amin proved to be a good administrator and a skilled politician and eventually emerged as a rising star in the Lebanese Christian community. Given the divisions and tensions in Lebanon, however, Amin's qualities as a politician were not always enough to assure him an easy ride. Eventually, he would find himself forced to confront the intractable problems that had come increasingly to characterize intercommunal relations in Lebanon since independence.

3

The Road to Civil War

In 1943, shortly before Lebanon gained its independence from France, parliamentary elections were held. The Constitutional Bloc party, led by a Maronite named Bishara al-Khuri, won by a considerable majority. Al-Khuri, who was a moderate, believed that an independent Lebanon would only be strong if the Sunni community enjoyed an adequate share of political power. In September 1943, following his election to the presidency, al-Khuri formed a new government, with Riad al-Sulh, the preeminent Sunni leader, serving as his prime minister. Al-Sulh, like al-Khuri, advocated cooperation between the Sunnis and the Maronites. The principles upon which the two men based the new government came to be known as the National Pact.

The National Pact represented a compromise between the views of the Maronites and those of the Sunnis. It was agreed that Lebanon should remain independent, sovereign, and neutral. In addition, the nation's Muslims would renounce the idea of unification with Syria or any other Arab nation; at the same time, the Christians, for their part, would neither pursue separatist policies nor seek to retain special ties with France or any other foreign power.

One difficulty [with the National Pact] arose from the fact that not all Lebanese communities were equally developed. . . . The politically aggressive Maronites got more than their just share of public office at the expense of the Greek Orthodox and other unaggressive Christian communities.
—KAMAL SALIBI
author

Lebanese president Camille Chamoun (right), meets with his prime minister, Sami al-Solh, during the crisis of 1958. Later, in the civil warfare that began in 1975, Chamoun would help found the Lebanese Front, a Maronite-led coalition that included the Kataib party and other Christian groups.

The Sixth Fleet of the U.S. Navy in the Beirut harbor in 1958. In July of that year, the pro-Western government in Iraq was overthrown. The American government, hoping to influence events in the region, then landed a large force of U.S. Marines in Lebanon.

As some people have put it, the Muslims accepted Lebanon's "Christian character" on condition that the Christians acknowledge Lebanon's "Arab face." Finally, al-Khuri and al-Sulh agreed to the distribution of parliamentary seats on the basis of five Muslim seats for every six Christian seats, with the presidency, premiership, and position of speaker of the parliament to be held by a Maronite, a Sunni, and a Shi'i, respectively.

The principles contained in the National Pact were never written out in an official document. Al-Sulh and al-Khuri did make some reference to them in speeches they gave later that year, but most Lebanese knew nothing of this arrangement, which the two men had arrived at without consulting the leaders of Lebanon's other sectarian communities, until 1946. The agreement reflected al-Khuri and al-Sulh's determination to prevent the secularization of Lebanese society and to further the interests of the *bourgeois*, or propertied, elements of the country's dominant communities.

During the first few years of Lebanese independence, Pierre Gemayel and the Kataib faced numerous problems, the most pressing of which was the question of how to define the movement now that its nationalist aspect had been rendered defunct by the country's changed circumstances. Gemayel and his aides eventually decided that the time had come to turn the movement into a conventional political party. An early move in this direction came in 1945, when a Kataib member stood for Parliament. In 1947 the party fielded four parliamentary candidates. That none of them won was of no great importance. What really mattered was that the party was gaining valuable political experience. It was also in 1947 that Pierre Gemayel announced that "representation is a means, not an end; we rejected it in the past because it had been corrupted; we look at it today as an ideal which serves the public in-

Gamal Abdel Nasser addresses a crowd during a visit to Algeria in 1963. Then president of Egypt, Nasser was the most popular leader of the Arab world. Though many Lebanese Muslims looked to Nasser for leadership, some Christian Lebanese deeply resented his policies and popularity.

Lebanese soldiers watch as a Beirut department store burns in 1958. The store was blown up by explosives hidden in a truck. In the civil war of the 1970s and 1980s, car bombs would become a gruesome part of the daily lives of all Lebanese.

terest . . . for us there are only two ways of serving the country: through legal electoral means or through violence. Although we firmly espouse the first method, we do not reject the second."

In the Lebanese general election of 1951, Pierre Gemayel stood as the Kataib candidate for the Metn and lost by a narrow margin. Three other Kataib candidates did secure election to Parliament, however, and the party went on to increase its representation at the next general election, which was held in 1957. By the end of the 1950s, the party had effectively begun to shed its image as an activist group. Gradually, the Kataib was gaining political legitimacy and respectability.

In 1956, Lebanese president Camille Chamoun, the leader of the National Liberal party (NLP), began to pursue a foreign policy the distinctly pro-Western nature of which represented a fundamental viola-

In 1958, a Lebanese woman reads a leaflet dropped by American airplanes over Beirut. The leaflets showed a picture of U.S. president Dwight D. Eisenhower and an explanation for the landing of American troops in Lebanon.

tion of the neutrality provisions of the National Pact. In October of that year, Great Britain, France, and Israel attacked Egypt. Britain and France's actions were a response to the decision taken by the immensely popular Egyptian President, Gamal Abdel Nasser, to nationalize the Suez Canal, which Britain and France had owned since 1875. Chamoun's refusal to censure Britain and France's hostile activities greatly angered many Lebanese Muslims, especially the Sunnis, whose denunciations of Chamoun were particularly uncompromising.

Chamoun's prestige sank still further in 1957, when he interfered in that year's general elections. His activities suggested that he hoped to pack the Lebanese Parliament with a majority of his own allies. In this way he hoped to amend the clause of the constitution that limits Lebanon's presidents to a single term of office. Chamoun's attempt to meddle with the democratic process appalled many of his compatriots. It was also in 1957 that Chamoun announced his support for the Eisenhower Doctrine, a policy initiative devised by U.S. president Dwight D. Eisenhower. The Eisenhower Doctrine recommended the use of U.S. forces to protect Middle Eastern states against aggression by any other nation "controlled by International Communism."

Lebanese policemen search a vehicle at a roadblock set up outside Beirut in July 1958. In September, the Kataib, under the leadership of Pierre Gemayel, led the Christian community against the new president, Fu'ad Shihab, in the bloodiest phase of the 1958 conflict.

The doctrine also proposed that the United States should offer economic aid and military advice to any Middle Eastern government that felt its independence threatened — in other words, to any Middle Eastern government that was prepared to back the United States in its ongoing diplomatic and ideological struggle against the Union of Soviet Socialist Republics (USSR). Chamoun's position on the Eisenhower Doctrine resulted in a spate of resignations from government officials.

During this period, Egypt and Syria reached an agreement that led to the formation of the United Arab Republic (UAR) in February 1958. The two countries would remain united until Syria's secession in 1961. At this time they were working for the establishment of a pro-Egyptian government in Lebanon. Many Lebanese political organizations, and especially the Kataib, were violently opposed to the UAR's policy. The Kataib viewed the UAR's machinations not only as a direct threat to Lebanese sovereignty but as a threat to the security of the Maronite community. Early in 1958, the leaders of the Druze and Muslim communities formed an alliance against Chamoun. A number of Christian leaders expressed their approval of the new coalition. Pierre Gemayel was one of the few Christian leaders who remained loyal to the government. Gemayel felt that if Chamoun and his government were overthrown, Lebanon's delicate political system would collapse. Accordingly, the Kataib declared its support for Chamoun.

By May 1958, civil strife had erupted throughout most of Lebanon, with opposition groups taking over nearly two-thirds of the country. At first, Chamoun ignored his enemies' demands that he resign. Then, in July, an Arab nationalist Iraqi army officer named Abdel Karim Kassem led a successful revolt against his country's reigning royal dynasty. Chamoun, fearing that the new Iraqi government might intervene in Lebanon in support of the Muslim rebels, asked for assistance from the U.S. government, which immediately sent 10,000 U.S. Marines to Beirut. Chamoun's self-serving overtures to the United

American troops aboard the U.S.S. *Upshur*, part of the large force sent to Lebanon in July 1958 by President Eisenhower. The Americans left a short time later in response to a United Nations resolution sponsored by a group of Arab states.

Large numbers of Palestinian refugees settled in Lebanon after fleeing their homes in 1948. By the 1960s, their camps were the centers of a growing Palestinian guerrilla movement. Many Lebanese, both Christian and Muslim, would later point to the activities of the guerrillas as a major cause of the civil war that broke out in 1975.

States completely destroyed what little credibility he still possessed in the eyes of most Lebanese. Under pressure from all quarters, the Lebanese president finally agreed that he would leave office at the end of his term, in September. When Chamoun stepped down, the presidency was assumed by Fu'ad Shihab, a well-respected former commander in chief of the Lebanese army who had won the support of many Lebanese by refusing to send in his troops to support the Chamoun government.

Although the Kataib had supported Chamoun, Pierre Gemayel kept his party's military involvement in the conflict to a minimum. Kataib militiamen fought to defend the Metn and to keep open the roads between the Metn and Beirut, where the Gemayels had numerous commercial and business interests they were determined to defend.

Following Chamoun's departure, relations between the Kataib and those groups that had opposed Chamoun remained tense. In September, when Fu'ad Haddad, an assistant editor of *al 'Amal*, the Kataib newspaper, was kidnapped, the Kataib responded by kidnapping a number of opposition leaders and organizing a general strike. The crisis intensified on September 24, when Shihab announced that Sunni leader Rashid Karami, who had led the revolt against Chamoun in Tripoli, would head the new cabinet. The other deputies who were awarded cabinet positions had also participated in the revolt or, failing that, had remained neutral. That the new cabinet contained no one who had supported Chamoun infuriated Gemayel, who also deeply distrusted both Shihab and Karami, believing them too closely associated with Egypt's President Nasser.

General Fu'ad Shihab, a former minister of Defense (left), succeeded Camille Chamoun (right) as Lebanon's president in 1958. Shihab was from a leading Lebanese clan that had ruled over Mount Lebanon in the 18th century.

Rashid Karami, a respected Sunni Muslim leader from the coastal city of Tripoli, was long considered one of the moderate voices in Lebanese politics. In 1987, while serving as prime minister under Amin Gemayel, Karami was assassinated.

Gemayel considered the preservation of Lebanon's independence and the Lebanese political system to be of paramount importance. Any threat to Lebanon, he believed, was a threat to the Maronite Christian homeland and, as such, was intolerable. Accordingly, the Kataib now launched a massive campaign of intimidation against the government. Open warfare between the Kataib and its opponents erupted throughout Lebanon, with both sides staging demonstrations and using kidnapping and murder as political weapons. The Kataib militia units fared well in battle, making effective use of their organizational abilities and maintaining excellent discipline even in the most disadvantageous situations.

After three weeks of mayhem, during which time the Kataib gained the support of many Lebanese Christians who had hitherto shown little or no regard for the party, the fighting, which had in many areas been largely between Muslims and Christians, ground to a halt. Intense negotiations between Shihab, Gemayel, Karami, and several other sectarian leaders eventually yielded an attempt at a political solution. Shihab announced the formation of a new, four-man "National Salvation Cabinet." Both Karami and Gemayel were chosen as members of the new cabinet, and Gemayel became minister of public works, education, and finance.

The rising power and prestige of the Kataib soon resulted in the party's achieving improved electoral showings. In the general election of 1960, six of the seven Kataib members who stood as candidates — including Pierre Gemayel, who ran in East Beirut — won seats in Parliament. The party was rapidly gaining both in popularity and, as many observers noted, in professionalism.

The Kataib now enjoyed representation both in the cabinet and in Parliament. Having attained this considerable measure of influence, the party began to take a more flexible approach in its endeavors to achieve those goals that it considered integral to the creation of a strong Lebanon. Throughout the late 1950s and early 1960s, Pierre Gemayel and other Kataib leaders pressed for economic and social reforms that would improve the living standards of the Lebanese. Perhaps the most significant of the reforms pushed through by the Kataib deputies and ministers was the institution of a social security code. The party had first begun to advocate the creation of the code in the early 1950s. The code, one of whose constituent measures provided for the payment of a small amount of money each month to retired workers, was promulgated by presidential decree in 1963 and came into effect in 1965.

The Kataib's political stance was quite conservative. It only approved of reforms that would not disturb the stability or structure of the existing political system. The party also took a conservative

In order to resolve the ongoing fighting in Lebanon in 1958, the new president, Fu'ad Shihab, appointed the four-man "Salvation Cabinet." The group included Pierre Gemayel (far right), and the prime minister, Rashid Karami (second from left).

position on economic issues, adhering firmly to principles of capitalism — the economic system based on private ownership and free enterprise. Like many Lebanese of his class and background, Pierre Gemayel was extremely proud of the vitality of Lebanon's capitalist economy. By the 1960s, Lebanon had become one of the Middle East's most prosperous and dynamic countries. Other Lebanese, however, pointed out that the country's wealth was unevenly distributed. For every prosperous Lebanese, there were many others who suffered from hunger and other forms of privation. Some of this criticism came from those who believed in socialism — the economic system that is based on government ownership of the means of production and seeks to bring about a more egalitarian distribution of wealth. For Gemayel, though, any radical change in the economic system represented a threat both to the established order and to the economic advantages that he and many Maronites were accustomed to enjoying. He therefore remained violently opposed to any attempt to radically change the economic system.

Kamal Jumblatt (center, with tie), the leader of the Druze community, with a group of his followers during the 1958 crisis. Jumblatt, who was a poet and mystic as well as a politician, was one of the dominant figures in Lebanese politics until his assassination in 1977.

Gemayel and many other Maronites were also deeply opposed to pan-Arabism, a political ideology that holds that all Arab states, including Lebanon, share a common identity. Many Maronites believe the Lebanese are not Arabs but a separate ethnic group. Their rejection of pan-Arabism also has religious overtones inasmuch as they consider pan-Arabism so closely linked with Islam that it would be impossible for Maronites to participate in the movement.

The Maronites' positions on politics and economics were greatly at variance with those of most other Lebanese. Many other sectarian factions, as well as a variety of leftist and other progressive movements, took a dim view of Maronite conservatism. Particularly galling to the Maronites' opponents was their refusal to contemplate a more equitable distribution of political power.

In 1960, Shihab, having clashed with other Maronite leaders, decided to ally himself with Pierre Gemayel, backing him in the general election that was held that year and making a considerable contribution to his victory. Gemayel then served in Shihab's cabinet until 1964, when new elections were

Israeli soldiers celebrate their victory over the Jordanian army, in June 1967, that led to the Israeli occupation of East Jerusalem and the West Bank. Behind them stands the Dome of the Holy Rock mosque. Muslims believe that in the 7th century the prophet Muhammad traveled from this site on a miraculous visit to Heaven.

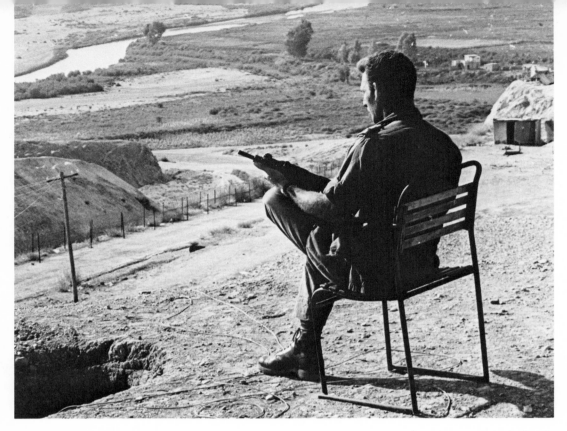

An Israeli soldier on guard duty near the Jordan River after the Israeli seizure of the West Bank in 1967. The defeat of the Arab armies in the Six-Day War was a humiliation for many Arabs and helped the Palestinian guerrilla movement win a large new following in Lebanon and other Arab states.

held. It was at this juncture that the Kataib leadership, eager to present the party as a national organization rather than merely the political arm of a single sect, decided that Gemayel should stand for the presidency. Only five deputies voted for Gemayel, but his attempt to gain the presidency, regardless of its largely symbolic nature, undoubtedly helped build his prestige.

In June 1967, Israel, responding to the massing of Arab troops on her borders, launched a preventive war, decisively defeating the armies and air forces of Jordan, Syria, and Egypt. The Lebanese military's decision not to get involved in the conflict greatly angered many Lebanese Muslims. It also infuriated Lebanon's Palestinian refugee population. PLO guerrillas based in camps in Lebanon had been sacrificing their lives in raids across the Israeli border for several years by this time, and many Palestinians in Lebanon saw the Lebanese army's nonparticipation in the war as a betrayal of their cause. As a result of the humiliating defeat that Israel had inflicted on the Arab nations' regular forces, many

Palestinians now began to give increased support to the guerrilla struggle.

In Lebanon, the PLO received a substantial amount of support from Druze and Muslim leaders and from several leftist political parties. Many other Lebanese, and the Maronites in particular, disliked the Palestinian presence. They especially resented that the Palestinians were forging links with some of Lebanon's most radical political factions and parties. These groups were becoming increasingly militant, pushing for sweeping changes in the political system and demanding that Lebanon play a greater role in the struggle against Israel.

In July 1967, Gemayel, Chamoun, and conservative Maronite leader Raymond Eddé issued a joint statement opposing radical demands that Lebanon sever diplomatic relations with Great Britain and the United States, which had supported Israel in the recent war. Gemayel argued that such a step would inevitably draw Lebanon into the conflict between Israel and its Arab neighbors. One month later, at the end of August, the three Maronite leaders announced that they would run in the 1968 general election at the head of a coalition to be known as the Triple Alliance.

The Triple Alliance was essentially a conservative Maronite reaction to the existing political situation. Gemayel and his two allies firmly believed that the growing strength of the PLO and Lebanon's indigenous radical movements represented a serious threat to Lebanon's traditional order. In turn, the Triple Alliance immediately came under concerted political attack from many non-Maronite Lebanese, including several Sunni leaders and a prominent Druze named Kamal Jumblatt, the leader of the Progressive Socialist party (PSP) and the founder of the Progressive Front. This was a coalition of leftist and other progressive groups that would later forge close alliances with several Palestinian organizations.

By the end of the 1960s, the Palestinian guerrillas were becoming increasingly aggressive within Lebanon. Some of them were even setting up checkpoints and collecting so-called donations from their Lebanese neighbors. At the same time, Israeli air

Lebanon is the only Arab country where the power of religious communities has practically succeeded in eliminating the state.
—AL-NAHAR
Lebanese scholar

and ground attacks on Palestinian positions in Lebanon became increasingly frequent. The Israelis claimed that they were only acting in retaliation against Palestinian raids on northern Israel. However, that many Lebanese were killed or wounded in the Israeli assaults indicated that the Israelis were determined to turn Lebanese opinion against the Palestinians. The Lebanese government, though under pressure from pro-Palestinian groups, usually did little to oppose the Israeli incursions. The troubled situation led to severe tensions between the Palestinians and the Lebanese government. However, on the few occasions when the Lebanese army fought the Palestinians, the guerrillas summoned reinforcements from camps in Syria and usually drove the Lebanese onto the defensive.

In 1969, at negotiations hosted by Nasser in Cairo, the PLO and the Lebanese government concluded a treaty, known as the Cairo Agreement. Under the terms of this agreement, PLO leader Yasir Arafat stated that his organization would neither attack Israel from bases in Lebanon nor involve itself in Lebanese affairs. In return, the Lebanese govern-

Imam Musa al-Sadr leads a vigil in a Beirut mosque in an attempt to stop the sectarian fighting in Lebanon in 1975. Sadr, an Iranian, was invited by the Shi'i of southern Lebanon in 1958 to replace the recently deceased religious head of the Shi'i community. A popular and controversial figure, Sadr disappeared during a visit to Libya in 1978.

ment agreed not to interfere with PLO supply lines between Lebanon and Syria and to relax its controls over the camps.

The Cairo Agreement appalled Gemayel and his colleagues, who accused the government of having relinquished its authority over the camps. Fearing that the government could no longer be trusted with protecting Lebanese sovereignty, Gemayel and other Christian leaders now decided to take matters into their own hands. In order to counter their opponents, the Kataib and other groups began to strengthen their respective militias and to recruit a new generation of adherents who would be willing to fight.

Another major development in Lebanon at this time was the rise of a powerful Shi'i political movement. By now, it was widely believed that the Shi'is constituted the largest single sectarian community in Lebanon. Prior to this period, the Shi'is had exercised little power. Their growing awareness of their unequal status now became a new and potent element in Lebanese politics. Under the leadership of the charismatic and respected Imam Musa al-Sadr, who had shown himself to be an articulate advocate of the Shi'i cause, the Shi'is now became a force with which to be reckoned. The Movement of the Disinherited, a radical Shi'i organization founded by al-Sadr, acquired great influence within the Shi'i community.

The growth of the Christian militias was paralleled by a massive increase in the number of militiamen that their opponents could field. Thousands of young Druze, Sunnis, and Shi'is now volunteered for service with the military arms of their respective political organizations. Some of these formations grew more powerful than the Lebanese army. The stage was now set for intercommunal strife on a scale never before witnessed in Lebanon. The tragedy of the situation was heightened by the fact that Israel and Syria would almost certainly become involved once the fighting started.

Civil war erupted in Lebanon in 1975. The Kataib struck the spark that many commentators believe was the immediate cause of the conflagration.

4

A Nation Torn Asunder

The Kataib leader who most historians believe was responsible for drawing the party into armed confrontation with the Palestinians and their Lebanese allies was Bashir Gemayel, Amin's younger brother. Bashir, who was born in 1947, had studied at the same schools as Amin. Following his graduation from the School of Law at the Université de St. Joseph, Bashir took a semester of postgraduate law studies at Southern Methodist University in Dallas, Texas, and later spent a brief period working for a law firm in Washington, D.C. Upon returning to Lebanon, he became heavily involved in the activities of the Kataib, whose military wing he had joined at age 11, during the crisis of 1958.

Many who knew Bashir have asserted that the young man was especially interested in the party's military activities. Bashir seems to have enjoyed the rigors of combat training and quickly became adept at handling firearms. He had an open and charismatic character that rapidly attracted a considerable circle of followers. Bashir also had a strong personality that often led him to make decisions on impulse rather than on careful deliberation. This would often land him in considerable trouble.

Those who knew Bashir well as an adolescent and young man found him an engaging but hardly striking person—except, that is, for a kind of freewheeling penchant he had for wild-eyed schemes, the more bloodthirsty the better.
—JONATHAN C. RANDAL
American journalist

Palestinian boys display a skull they found in a Beirut building destroyed in the fighting of 1975. That spring, Kataib gunmen fired on a busload of civilian Palestinians and Lebanese in the Ayn al-Rumani neighborhood of Beirut. This event is considered the starting point of the civil war.

In 1969, Pierre Gemayel appointed Bashir to lead a 100-man Kataib militia unit. On March 23, 1970, Bashir and his men conducted their first major action against the Palestinians. They ambushed a Palestinian convoy in the Metn, in a village on the highway that connects Beirut with the Syrian capital, Damascus. Bashir's unit killed 10 Palestinians. During the next two weeks, other Kataib militia units went into action against Palestinian formations elsewhere in the Metn and in parts of Beirut. On March 25, PLO guerrillas kidnapped Bashir and briefly held him prisoner in the Tel al-Za'tar refugee camp. Following negotiations between Arafat and Jumblatt, Bashir was released.

Bashir's hostility toward the Palestinians was much more intense than his father's. Pierre Gemayel, though opposed to the PLO's activities in Lebanon, does seem to have been sensitive to the Palestinians' plight; at no point in his career did he ever call for the outright expulsion of all Palestinians from Lebanon. As far as Bashir was concerned, however, the sooner the Palestinians were driven out of Lebanon, the better.

The Kataib excess that triggered the Lebanese civil war burst upon the tense and nervous nation in 1975. On April 13, as Pierre Gemayel and his entourage were leaving a church in Beirut's predominantly Maronite Ayn al-Rumani neighborhood, armed men opened fire from a passing car. Four people were killed, including two Kataib members and Pierre Gemayel's bodyguard, Joseph Abu Asi. Firmly convinced that the assassins were Palestinian, Kataib militiamen struck back an hour later. They attacked a bus carrying Palestinians and Lebanese to the Tel al-Za'tar neighborhood. News of the shooting, which left 27 innocent people dead and 19 others wounded, spread quickly, and within days fighting had broken out in several parts of Beirut, mainly around the camps. In the Naba' area, Maronite militiamen fought armed members of the Communist party of Lebanon (CPL). In the slum areas of Karantina and Maslakh, the Kataib battled groups of Shi'i and Syrian fighters. By April 18, the fighting had claimed more than 300 lives and left more than 1,500 buildings destroyed or seriously damaged.

The war in the streets naturally had repercussions in Parliament. Prime Minister Rashid Solh, a member of a leading Sunni family and one of the country's more liberal politicians, pressured Pierre Gemayel to turn over to the government a group of Kataib activists who were suspected of involvement in the attack on the bus. Gemayel, determined to protect his followers and his own authority as leader of the Kataib, refused. Further discussion of the problem proved fruitless, and several Kataib and NLP ministers then resigned from their posts, precipitating both the collapse of the cabinet and Solh's resignation.

Up until December 1975, the fighting in Lebanon was mainly among the Lebanese themselves. The

Bashir Gemayel, a charismatic, forceful leader, became the hero of the Maronite Christian community. He was hated and distrusted by many other Lebanese, however, partly for his cooperation with the Israeli army during its invasion of Lebanon in the summer of 1982.

Suleiman Franjieh served as Lebanon's president from 1970 to 1976. In June 1978, a group of Kataib fighters attacked the Franjieh summer estate in Ehden and killed Franjieh's son Tony as well as Tony's wife, their young daughter, and a number of Franjieh's followers.

Kataib was allied with the militias of Chamoun and another Maronite leader, Suleiman Franjieh, then the increasingly unpopular president of Lebanon. They fought the forces of the National Movement — the successor organization to the Progressive Front — and the National Movement's close ally, al-Amal, a Shi'i militia established by al-Sadr's followers.

In January 1976, Christian militiamen laid siege to the Palestinian camps of Tel al-Za'tar and Dubayeh. More than 50 people were massacred by Christian militiamen in Tel al-Za'tar when it fell. In response to the Maronite atrocities, Arafat, who until now had kept the PLO's guerrillas out of the fighting, ordered his men into battle alongside the National Movement. Aided by the PLO, whose guerrillas were experienced fighters, the National Movement rapidly gained the upper hand. They overran large areas of West Beirut and captured Damur, Chamoun's hometown, which is situated on the Lebanese coast.

By March 1976, the Christian militias had been forced onto the defensive. At the same time, the Lebanese army began to fall apart as soldiers and officers deserted and went off to join the militias of their respective communities. With the disintegration of the army, Franjieh's government became a fiction. On May 8, 1976, another Maronite leader, Elyas Sarkis, was elected as the new president. Just before the end of Franjieh's term in March, Syria, which had been watching the deterioration of the situation in Lebanon with growing alarm, decided to intervene. Syria's president Hafez al-Asad — the leader of the ruling Ba'th Socialist party — and his colleagues were determined to prevent the defeat of the Christians and the overthrow of the Lebanese government. The Syrians feared that such developments would lead to the creation of a radical Leb-

A masked Kataib fighter behind sandbags during the attack on the Palestinian Tel al-Za'tar refugee camp in 1976. For more than 50 days Christian forces laid siege to the camp. After the exhausted inhabitants surrendered, the Christian fighters massacred a number of them.

A member of the Kataib militia poses on an armed truck captured from Palestinian guerrillas during the fighting around the Karantina refugee camp in 1976. The Kataib leadership and many other Lebanese viewed the Palestinians as a leading cause of the political troubles in Lebanon in the 1960s and 1970s.

anon enjoying the backing of the PLO, an organization for which the Syrian regime had little affection.

Syrian troops began entering Lebanon in March 1976 and quickly set about securing control over the Palestinians and their Lebanese allies. The Syrians also worked to bolster the Christian militias. By October of that same year, the al-Asad regime had more than 30,000 troops in Lebanon and had won the official approval of other Arab states for its presence there. Because the Israelis had made it clear that they considered the stability of that part of Lebanon that lies to the south of the Litani River vital to their interests, the Syrians kept their forces out of that region. The Litani River thus became the effective line of demarcation between the Syrian and Israeli spheres of influence in Lebanon.

In June 1976, the Kataib, the Chamounist militia, and a number of other Christian militias decided to work in closer concert. Together, they laid siege to the Tel al-Za'tar camp. The fighting raged for more than 50 days, during which time the attackers frequently managed to sever the Palestinians' supply lines. This forced the Palestinians to defend themselves while trying to cope with critical shortages of food and medicine. The camp eventually fell on August 12, when Arafat's lieutenants were still negotiating with the Kataib in hopes of arranging an orderly evacuation. Historian Tabitha Petran gives a chilling account of what happened next: "Rightist forces deliberately stormed the camp before these arrangements could be carried out — if, indeed, the [Kataib] ever intended them to be carried out — and also tricked the camp population into coming out into the open to face their fire. . . . Entire families were killed. There was hardly a male between the ages of ten and fifty among those who managed to reach West Beirut. Boys of eight and ten were summarily executed. Girls no older than that were raped before being dispatched. All sixty camp nurses, women and men, were lined up two

Syrian troops enter the Lebanese port city of Sidon in the spring of 1976. A string of victories by the Palestinian-leftist coalition over the Christian forces alarmed the Syrian leadership. In order to prevent the creation of a radical state in Lebanon, the Syrians sent in a large army that soon occupied much of the country.

Bashir Gemayel (right), Lebanon's newly elected president, greets his predecessor, Elyas Sarkis, in August 1982. For months Bashir had attempted to portray himself as a moderate, a man who would serve not just the Maronite community but all other Lebanese as well.

by two, marched out, and machine-gunned. Looters — often families of the killers — wore masks to protect themselves from the stench of rotting corpses." More than 3,000 Palestinians and Lebanese died in the massacre.

The siege of Tel al-Za'tar also resulted in Bashir Gemayel's accession to greater power within the Kataib. On July 13, a Palestinian sniper shot and killed William Hawi, the commander of the Kataib's military wing. After some hesitation, which was based on their misgivings concerning Bashir's impulsiveness, Pierre Gemayel and Amin Gemayel decided to appoint Bashir as Hawi's replacement.

In August 1976, four right-wing Christian militias, including the Kataib, established a collective command structure. This new organization adopted the name al-Quwat al-Lubnaniyah, or the Lebanese Forces. This organization was initially to be the military arm of the Lebanese Front, a political coalition that had been founded a few months earlier by a group of Christian leaders. These included Pierre Gemayel, Chamoun, and Father Bulus Na'-man, the head of the permanent congress of the Lebanese monastic orders. The program of the Lebanese Front proposed that Lebanon should remain a united republic, that some changes would have to be made in the National Pact to achieve this, and that the country should be reorganized on a federal basis. It also stated that the Palestinians should not be allowed to settle on Lebanese soil. The members of the Lebanese Front refused, however, to contemplate even the slightest change in the position of the Maronites within the Lebanese political system. Their attitude in this respect made the perpetuation of conflict inevitable.

At first, the Lebanese Forces created integrated units from its constituent militias, with the militias

Tensions between the Syrian army and the Maronite militias led to the Syrian shelling of parts of East Beirut in July 1978. The Lebanese Christian forces had welcomed the Syrians at first because they had prevented Palestinian and leftist forces from taking power in Lebanon.

Hafez al-Asad, president of Syria, confers with Yasir Arafat, the head of the Palestine Liberation Organization (PLO), in 1976. At a summit conference in Riyadh, Saudi Arabia, Arab leaders had approved the Syrian peacekeeping role in Lebanon. Syria had sent in 30,000 troops in an attempt to quell the fighting there.

themselves remaining separate from these units. At the same time, however, Bashir Gemayel decided to consolidate his authority, by armed force if necessary, over the other Christian militias. Many of the actions he undertook in pursuit of this aim were criticized by Maronite moderates. One action in particular, conducted specifically against the Franjieh family and its militia, earned Bashir widespread condemnation.

The Gemayels and the Franjiehs had been rivals for many years. Suleiman Franjieh, the former president and a leading Maronite za'im, had wanted nothing to do with the Lebanese Forces. He had refused to allow his militia, the Marada Brigade, to join the organization. In June 1978, a force of 600 Kataib fighters led by Bashir's lieutenant Samir Ja'ja' attacked Ehden, the Franjieh family's summer estate. In the fighting Suleiman Franjieh's son, Tony, Tony's wife, and the couple's three-year-old daughter were killed along with a number of other people.

Pierre Gemayel and Amin Gemayel are said to have been outraged by the Ehden massacre. From that point on, they attempted to curb Bashir's powers. It was not long, however, before Bashir began to demonstrate that he was no longer under his family's control. Bashir now had his own power base — the Lebanese Forces. Even though most of its members belonged to the Kataib, the Lebanese Forces itself enjoyed considerable autonomy from that organization.

It was also in 1978 that the situation on the border between Lebanon and Israel deteriorated. In response to a particularly violent raid on Israel by PLO guerrillas based in Lebanon, the IDF invaded. The PLO guerrillas, heavily outnumbered and possessing no weaponry as sophisticated as that of the Israelis, mounted a remarkably effective resistance for six days and then withdrew, having sustained only minimal casualties. That Israeli artillery fire and aerial bombing killed nearly 2,000 Lebanese civilians and approximately 500 Palestinian noncombatants represented an early instance of the pattern of indiscriminate killing that would eventually come to characterize most Israeli military actions in Lebanon. Writing of the destruction wrought by the Israelis in the area between Tyre and Mount Hermon, H. D. S. Greenway, a reporter for the *Washington Post*, noted: "There is hardly a town left undamaged. Some have been all but flattened by air strikes and shelling. . . . The damage belies Israel's claims of surgical strikes against Palestinian bases and camps."

Bashir Gemayel and troops from the Lebanese Forces ride in a tank through East Beirut. By the early 1970s, Lebanon was a prosperous arms market; weapons of all kinds, obtained primarily from the United States and Europe, were sold there by arms merchants.

Kamal Jumblatt, the Druze leader and head of a coalition of leftist Lebanese groups, lies in state, along with his driver and bodyguard, after his assassination in 1977. Jumblatt was shot after passing trough a Syrian checkpoint near Beirut.

International condemnation eventually resulted in an Israeli withdrawal, and the UN established a peacekeeping force — the Interim Force in Lebanon, commonly referred to as UNIFIL — to curb the guerrilla raids on Israel. The Israelis, skeptical of UNIFIL's ability to fulfill its mission, established a buffer zone of their own in southern Lebanon by arming and supplying local Christian forces led by Major Sa'd Haddad, a renegade Lebanese army officer. In July 1979, Haddad proclaimed the area under his control "independent free Lebanon."

During this period, the Lebanese Forces frequently came into conflict with the Syrians, who were becoming increasingly nervous about the strength of the Lebanese military. Even though the Syrians had entered the country to help the Maronites, Bashir Gemayel and other hard-line Maronite rightists eventually began demanding that the Syrians withdraw. In 1978 and 1979, the Syrians attempted to intimidate the Lebanese Forces, shelling Ashrafiyah, a Maronite enclave in East Beirut, and causing considerable destruction of property and loss of life.

By the end of the 1970s, Lebanon's Maronite heartland had achieved a considerable measure of

In 1978, Major Sa'd Haddad, a renegade Lebanese Army officer, organized a militia in the south of Lebanon that became a surrogate security force for Israel. Haddad died of cancer in 1984, but the militia, called the South Lebanon Army, still exists, trained and equipped by the Israelis.

autonomy. Conservative Maronites like the Gemayels had, in effect, created a Maronite ministate; many people had by now begun to refer to it as "Marunistan." This region, centered on the city of Jounieh, covers an area of about 800 square miles. It has its own administrative apparatus, port facilities, airport, and tax system.

The rise of Marunistan was a powerful indication of the extent to which many Maronites had become convinced that Christian Lebanon should stand apart from the rest of the country. The Gemayels undoubtedly supported the move toward autonomy, but they do not seem to have agreed with those Maronites who, taking a more extreme view, spoke of the creation of Greater Lebanon in the 1920s as having been a terrible mistake. Pierre Gemayel himself remained a strict Lebanese nationalist.

The next operation that Bashir Gemayel masterminded in his drive for political and military supremacy within the Maronite community was directed against Chamoun's militia, the Tigers. On July 7, 1980, the Lebanese Forces went into battle against the Tigers. After heavy fighting they emerged victorious. With this action, the Lebanese Forces gained overwhelming superiority throughout the Maronite heartland; the organization now controlled the major ports, assumed responsibility for security and public order, and managed the region's main business enterprises, including a wide variety of illegal commercial operations such as drug smuggling. Bashir Gemayel had now become the dominant Maronite leader.

Pierre Gemayel recovers from a bomb attack on his car in 1979 that left 1 person dead and 14 others wounded. Though in his mid-70s, Gemayel continued to exert great influence on the Kataib party and on the Maronite community in general.

On June 6, 1982, the Israelis, using the shooting of their ambassador to Great Britain as a pretext, launched a massive invasion of Lebanon with the intention of driving the PLO out of that country altogether. The Palestinians fought back hard, but the more powerful IDF continued to batter its way northward. By June 15 the Israelis had Beirut surrounded. Following negotiations by American, Saudi, and European envoys, it was agreed that the PLO would withdraw its forces from Lebanon.

The Israeli invasion had proved incredibly destructive, devastating large areas of Beirut and several other major cities. Thousands of Lebanese and Palestinians were killed, and tens of thousands more were left homeless. During the siege of the camps in West Beirut, the Israelis had cut off the area's water and electricity supplies, thus inflicting terrible suffering on combatants and noncombatants alike.

Bashir Gemayel waves to supporters minutes after being elected president. Despite attempts to present himself as a moderate leader who had the future of all of Lebanon in mind, Bashir was still distrusted by most non-Maronite Lebanese.

Menachem Begin, the prime minister of Israel from 1977 to 1983, holds a press conference in Washington, D.C., in 1981. In the summer of 1982, Begin and his defense minister, Ariel Sharon, launched an invasion of Lebanon that culminated in the siege of Beirut.

Many Maronites, however, welcomed the Israeli intervention. In addition to forcing Arafat and the PLO out of Lebanon, the IDF had also severely mauled the PLO's Lebanese leftist allies. Many Maronites believed that they could now reassert their authority over the country. The Israeli government, for its part, had shipped arms and equipment to the Maronites on numerous occasions during the previous three decades and was now eager to create a new, Maronite-dominated political order in Lebanon. The Israelis believed that a Maronite ascendancy in Lebanon would be the best possible guarantee of security for Israel's northern border.

During the invasion, the Israelis had made effective use of their links with Bashir Gemayel, which had first begun to be forged early in the 1970s. The Lebanese Forces assisted the IDF in the blockade of West Beirut and helped the Israeli occupation forces in several other cities. Like many other Maronites, Bashir was delighted by the punishment the Israelis had inflicted on the Palestinians.

In June 1982, Bashir, who had begun seeking to portray himself as a national leader rather than simply as the head of a single community, announced that he would stand as a candidate for the presidency. He called for the departure of all foreign troops from Lebanon and emphasized the need for a strong Lebanese government. His critics remained skeptical, however. The Druze, Sunni, and Shi'i leaders, infuriated by Bashir's support of the Israelis during the invasion, called upon their parliamentary deputies to boycott the election. The election was held on August 23 in a military barracks in an Israeli-controlled area just outside Beirut. Only a handful of Druze and Muslim deputies attended, and some time passed before a quorum was achieved. On the second ballot, 57 of the 62 deputies present voted for Bashir, who thus became president.

Bashir's victory delighted his Maronite followers. The Israelis also voiced their approval, and Israeli prime minister Menachem Begin sent a telegram congratulating Bashir. Most of Lebanon's other communities either ignored the election or violently denounced it. Bashir, hoping to mollify his critics, continued to act in a conciliatory manner. He was

Lebanese rescue workers remove the dead from the Palestinian camp of Sabra. In September 1982, fighters from the Lebanese Forces and the South Lebanon Army, assisted by Israeli officers, entered Sabra and the neighboring camp of Shatila and massacred hundreds of innocent Palestinians.

not, however, to have much time in which to convince his critics that he intended to serve as the leader of all Lebanese rather than just the Maronites. On September 14, he was assassinated. The Israelis, claiming that they merely wanted to forestall any intercommunal violence that might arise as a result of the assassination, immediately seized West Beirut, in direct contravention of a previous agreement with the Lebanese government.

On September 16, Lebanese Forces units entered the Sabra and Shatila camps in West Beirut with Israeli assistance. The massacre that followed would last for more than 36 hours and result in the death of an estimated 2,500 Palestinians and 700 Lebanese. The IDF troops in the area, many of whom later reported that their officers had ordered them not to get involved, remained outside the camps and did nothing to stop the killing, whose perpetrators

A Palestinian fighter prepares to board a ship in Beirut during the evacuation of Palestinian guerrillas from Lebanon in 1982. The evacuation followed the Israeli siege of Beirut and difficult rounds of negotiations between the Israelis, Palestinians, and American envoys.

— along with the local Israeli commanders and their political masters in the Israeli cabinet — portrayed the massacre as an antiterrorist operation. Israeli general Ariel Sharon insisted that there were "2,000 terrorists" hiding in Sabra and Shatila.

There were, in fact, no terrorists at all in the camps, and Sharon and his colleagues knew it. As part of their ongoing campaign to write the entire Palestinian people as well as the PLO out of the Middle Eastern political equation, Israel's political and military leaders had elected to allow the Lebanese Forces to avenge Bashir's death by murdering Palestinian civilians.

The International Commission that was later established to investigate the massacre concluded that Israeli and Kataib claims of a terrorist presence in the camps were false. The Commission noted in its report that "there was absolutely no resistance to the massacres. . . . The militiamen suffered virtually no casualties in their execution of the massacres . . . an Oxfam [relief agency] worker cites a sporting pellet gun lying beside the corpse of a young boy as epitomizing the total defenselessness of the camp population."

When the killing was over, most of the houses in the camps, many of which still contained the corpses of victims, were bulldozed. On September 21, Amin Gemayel was elected president of Lebanon, winning the votes of 77 of the 80 deputies who participated in the election.

Bashir Gemayel accompanies an American marine sergeant in a review of the Italian contingent of the multinational peacekeeping forces in Beirut. The American, French, and Italian forces came to Lebanon to assist in the evacuation of Palestinian fighters from Beirut in August 1982.

5

A Man for All Communities?

Those groups that had fought the Gemayels in the civil war considered Amin a more attractive figure than his brother. Amin enjoyed fairly good relations with several Druze and Muslim leaders, and he was not as closely identified as his brother with the worst violence of the war. In light of these considerations, there were a number of non-Maronite Lebanese who took a positive view of the new president. They hoped that Amin would prove to be a leader for the country as a whole, not just for the Maronites.

Amin's inaugural address, which he delivered on September 23, 1982, showed a desire to achieve a measure of reconciliation with Lebanon's non-Maronite communities. Having first praised Bashir and his predecessor, Elyas Sarkis, Amin declared: "I speak as a member of this House and as a man of the people, our great people among whom I was brought up, whose sufferings I have shared and whose cause I have always defended and championed. I say to you, therefore, that I shall join with you in this great process of national restoration."

I am deeply conscious of the aspirations of my people and the needs of my country. The country is in dire need of national solidarity and a staunch affirmation of unity which will shield us from the many dangers that threaten us. Without national unity, there is no nation.
—AMIN GEMAYEL

Amin Gemayel and U.S. president Ronald Reagan give brief statements to the press at the end of Gemayel's visit to Washington, D.C., in December 1983. Gemayel stressed the need to end the occupation of Lebanese territory by the Syrian and Israeli armies. He also won U.S. support for his efforts to end the fighting in Lebanon.

Nabih Beri addresses a rally in the Lebanese town of Baalbak in 1985. Beri, a lawyer, assumed control of the Shi'i political movement, al-Amal, after its founder, Imam Musa al-Sadr, disappeared in 1978. Behind him is a picture of the Iranian leader Ayatollah Khomeini.

In his address, Amin also stressed the need for national unity and for the rebuilding of all that had been destroyed. Within a matter of weeks, however, it became apparent to many people — and especially to the Muslims — that Amin had little intention of seeking reconciliation. One particularly stark example of his true position was his blunt refusal to meet with Nabih Beri, a lawyer and the leader of the Shi'i militia, al-Amal, just a month after his inauguration. Amin knew perfectly well that the al-Amal leadership was sincerely committed to the restoration of Lebanese sovereignty, but as American historian Augustus Richard Norton recounts in his essay "Estrangement and Fragmentation in Lebanon," when Beri asked for an interview with Amin, one of Amin's closest advisers informed Beri that "the President is not seeing any lawyers."

Maronite reaction to Amin's election was positive. He had shown himself to be a dedicated spokesman for his community in Parliament, and in the clashes of 1975 he had also demonstrated that he was capable of fighting courageously. Some Maronites, however, were not particularly enamored of Amin. The Lebanese Forces in particular distrusted his political views, especially his moderate stand on many issues and his relatively amicable relations with Muslim and Palestinian leaders.

Amin faced numerous problems that can only be described as daunting. Seven years of civil war and two Israeli invasions had devastated much of the country. There were few Lebanese families that had not lost at least one member to the violence. Israeli shells and the years of intersectarian fighting had reduced whole neighborhoods in Beirut and several other cities to ruins. It was estimated that by the time the Israeli invasion of 1982 ended more than 72,000 Lebanese homes had been damaged or completely destroyed. As a result, many thousands of Lebanese as well as Palestinians were now homeless.

In 1983, workers rebuild a Beirut neighborhood. Years of fighting in Lebanon have resulted in massive destruction of property. Few areas of the country have been spared, and, frequently, renewed fighting in one area or another has resulted in the devastation of newly rebuilt buildings and homes.

The war years had also dealt a traumatic blow to the Lebanese economy. Prior to the invasion, the economy had generally managed to stay afloat even in the most difficult circumstances. Although the civil war had brought about a massive reduction in government revenues, most banking and investment enterprises had remained viable. Some of them had even managed to thrive. After the invasion, however, the economy simply collapsed. Investments shrank, industry contracted, and government debt soared. Perhaps most serious was the sharp fall in the value of the Lebanese pound (LL), which had held steady through the years of conflict prior to 1980. The economy of southern Lebanon had suffered particularly badly during the years of warfare between the PLO and the Israelis before the invasion. When the area came under Israeli control in the wake of the invasion, its economic situation became immeasurably worse.

A poster exhibited in Baghdad, Iraq, in 1980 shows Begin, Assad, and Khomeini — the leaders of Israel, Syria, and Iran — under pressure from the United States to leave Lebanon. Foreign interference in Lebanese affairs has been a problem for Lebanon throughout its history.

Another major problem that Amin had to face was the presence of the Syrian and Israeli armies on Lebanese soil. Both Syria and Israel enjoyed the advantages of superpower support, with the United States giving massive financial, military, and diplomatic support to Israel, and the USSR fulfilling a similar role in relation to Syria. Israel and Syria had been rivals for many years, and both countries felt that they had vital interests at stake in Lebanon. As a result, any move that one of the countries made in Lebanon usually provoked a countermove by the other. Much of this maneuvering was conducted by the two countries' respective Lebanese allies.

Perhaps the most intractable problem confronting Amin was the widespread conflict between the various Lebanese communities, especially that between the Maronites and their opponents. Many non-Maronite radical and moderate groups continued to call for changes in the political system that the Maronites, for their part, were completely unwilling to accept. Most non-Maronite Lebanese believed that the Maronites' political supremacy was no longer justified. The Maronite community was no longer in the majority, and its top politicians had

In September 1983, Christian militiamen shell Druze military positions in the Shuf mountains. After the Israeli occupation of the Shuf in 1982, the Lebanese Forces set up positions there in an attempt to expand their area of control. This led to clashes between those forces and the Druze.

الرئيس الشيخ أمين الجميّل

Israeli military vehicles pass by a picture of Amin Gemayel. The Israel Defense Forces (IDF) withdrew from the Shuf area in 1983 as fighting between the Druze and the Lebanese Forces continued. Many observers felt that the IDF had deliberately set up the fighting by allowing the Lebanese Forces to establish garrisons in the area in 1982.

shown themselves incapable of providing effective leadership at the national level.

It was not long before Amin began to disappoint whatever hopes Lebanon's non-Maronites might originally have had in him. In many ways, he demonstrated that he shared his fellow Maronites' unwillingness to consider changing the political system. Soon after he became president, Amin formed a government in which the majority of the most important positions went to members of the Kataib. Some have claimed that in doing this Amin merely followed an established tradition in Lebanese politics; others, however, contend that Amin exceeded what was generally considered acceptable within that tradition. His critics accused him of trying to establish a Maronite hegemony over the government. Amin also appointed his followers to important positions in several labor unions and professional organizations and ensured that the army, which had begun to reconstitute itself in the wake of the civil war, would be led by men who were loyal both to the Kataib and to him personally.

Criticism of Amin's policies regarding the army was especially widespread. Soon after the PLO's withdrawal from Beirut and shortly before the massacres at Sabra and Shatila, units of the Lebanese army moved into Beirut. Initially, most people accepted this as a sign of a return to normalcy, as a legitimate aspect of the government's effort to reassert its authority. However, the army soon began to show that it was serving Maronite interests as well as those of the state. Soldiers began arresting Palestinians and Lebanese radicals, many of whom were then imprisoned in East Beirut. The army also moved against the poorer Shi'i neighborhoods, destroying many houses and arresting a large number of people. Many Lebanese bitterly resented the army's lack of effort in East Beirut to control the Kataib militia and the Lebanese Forces, both of which continued to act as illegally and brutally as they had during the civil war and the Israeli invasion.

Honor guards stand over coffins of 15 U.S. Marines killed in Beirut in October 1983. They and 226 other Americans died when a truck loaded with explosives blew up next to the Marine headquarters outside Beirut.

Druze fighters celebrate their victory over the Lebanese army in the mountain village of Kbar Shamun in February 1984. The Druze, always sensitive to the presence of non-Druze in their area of the Shuf, had not only defeated government troops but in earlier battles had also routed the Lebanese Forces.

Even if Amin had wanted to introduce changes in the political system, it is unlikely that he would have been able to do so. Most of his fellow Maronites, and particularly the hard-liners, were determined to make sure that no such changes took place.

Of the hard-line Maronite groups that distrusted Amin, the Lebanese Forces, which was now the principal power in Marunistan, undoubtedly represented the most serious challenge to Amin's attempt to emerge as a bona fide national leader. Amin realized that he was in no position to challenge the Lebanese Forces militarily even if he wanted to — the Lebanese Forces had become a much more effective fighting organization than the struggling Lebanese army.

After the Israeli invasion ended, the Lebanese Forces embarked on a series of operations intended to extend their control in several parts of the country. Assisted by the Israelis, they met with considerable success at first. Eventually, however, their efforts provoked a violent reaction from other Lebanese groups. During the last months of 1982 and the early months of 1983, units of the Lebanese Forces, supported by the IDF, moved into the mountainous Shuf region, which lies to the south and east of Beirut. There they established garrisons in Aley and several other towns. Skirmishes between

A Shi'i fighter of the al-Amal militia wears a Santa Claus mask during fighting against the Lebanese Army in Beirut. In 1983, the army launched an attack on Muslim neighborhoods in West Beirut in an attempt to extend government control over the capital city.

the Lebanese Forces and local Druze militia units soon became frequent. In late August of 1983, when the IDF withdrew from the region, the fighting intensified. The Druze, who, as Israeli historian Itamar Rabinovich notes in *The War for Lebanon, 1970–1985*, "enjoy a political influence well beyond their numerical strength" because of their "territorial concentration, solidarity, military skill, and political acumen," proved formidable adversaries. They not only routed the Lebanese Forces but inflicted a humiliating defeat on the Lebanese army units that the government sent out to stop the fighting.

By April 1983, the government of the United States was playing an active role in negotiations to persuade Amin to sign an accord with Israel. Begin and Sharon had been pressing the Lebanese government for an accord since the first weeks of the invasion. The U.S. government, which was strongly

Shi'i leader Nabih Beri confers with Walid Jumblatt, who took over the leadership of the Druze after his father's assassination in 1977. They and other Lebanese leaders met in Switzerland in 1983 and 1984 in two rounds of fruitless talks aimed at reconciliation between the various Lebanese communities.

pro-Israel, now began to exert its considerable political and diplomatic strength toward the same end. U.S. president Ronald Reagan's administration had by this time abandoned its earlier policy of presenting itself as an impartial actor in the Lebanese crisis. About 1,200 U.S. Marines had arrived in Lebanon following the Sabra and Shatila massacres, ostensibly to act as a peacekeeping force. Most non-Maronite Lebanese soon realized that the United States, with its long history of support for Israel and opposition to Arab radicalism, was, in fact, backing Lebanon's almost exclusively Maronite and profoundly conservative government. In their eyes the U.S. was trying to ensure that Lebanon would remain solidly pro-Western. The U.S. government was also determined to counter Syrian influence in the area because Syria enjoyed the backing of the USSR, the United States' principal rival.

In May 1983, Amin finally agreed to sign an accord with Israel. The agreement provided for, among other things, Israel's withdrawal from Lebanon. The Israeli withdrawal was made contingent, however, on the withdrawal of Syrian and Palestinian troops from Lebanon. On May 14 the Lebanese cabinet voted unanimously to accept the terms of the accord, which was duly signed three days later. Ratification of the accord proved problematic, however. Throughout the summer and fall of 1983, opposition to the accord intensified. The majority of Lebanese, including a number of Maronites, were extremely critical of the agreement. The Syrian regime considered the accord completely unacceptable and immediately began trying to persuade Amin to annul it. To make their position clear, the Syrians began to exert pressure on Amin's government via their military proxies in Lebanon: the Druze, Sunni, and Shi'i militias.

That U.S. policy in Lebanon was doomed to fail by reason of its partisan nature became increasingly apparent throughout 1983. In April of that year, the U.S. embassy in Beirut was blown up. In September, the United States, having already assembled a large naval task force off the Lebanese coast, sent a further 2,000 marines to Lebanon. That same month,

Serious as external manipulations of the Lebanese scene have been, however, and important as support for the left from radical states has been, the greatest danger to the Lebanese entity has proven to be the Palestinian presence on its soil.
—DAVID C. GORDON
American historian

Members of the Lebanese Forces disassemble a mortar in a neighborhood of East Beirut in July 1984. In an attempt to stop the fighting between Muslim, Druze, and Christian militias, the Lebanese army was deployed throughout the capital city.

U.S. vice-president George Bush made the Reagan administration's position particularly clear by demanding that Syria "get out of Lebanon." The U.S. Department of Defense asserted that the military buildup in the eastern Mediterranean had been effected in order to "send a message to Syria." For many observers it was evident that the American government was trying to tilt the balance of power in favor of Amin Gemayel and away from the Syrians and their Lebanese allies.

U.S. military personnel provided logistic support to the Lebanese army throughout September, frequently directing U.S. naval gunfire onto Druze positions in the Shuf. The governments of Great Britain, France, and Italy, which had also sent peacekeeping forces to Lebanon, urged the Reagan administration to confine its activities in Lebanon to protecting Lebanese civilians and to stop supporting what they saw as the Gemayel government's assault on its own people. The Reagan administration refused to alter its position. On October 24 it paid for its intransigence. A suicide squad drove a truck filled with explosives into the marine headquarters in Beirut. The explosion killed 241 marines. Just moments later, a similar attack on the headquarters of the French peacekeeping force killed 50 soldiers.

The identity of the organization responsible for the assaults remains unknown. A former al-Sadr lieutenant, Hussein Musawi, declared that the attackers were "the orphans and widows of the victims and martyrs of Sabra and Shatila, of Beirut's southern suburbs and of north and south Lebanon." His statement is powerful evidence that the marines died at the hands of Lebanese who opposed their country's U.S.-supported government.

The elderly statesman Pierre Gemayel greets the press in 1984. That August, Gemayel died of a heart attack after attending a cabinet meeting. His death at age 78 came as a blow to Amin Gemayel, who had depended a great deal upon the support of his father against more radical factions in the Maronite community.

Israeli troops stand guard over the Ain Hilweh Palestinian camp outside of Sidon in 1984. Israeli air and land attacks on Palestinian camps and military positions in southern Lebanon continued through the 1980s.

By February 1984, the Druze had occupied every town in the Shuf except Suq al-Gharb. The fighting, which had occasionally been extremely heavy, resulted in the displacement of thousands of Christians whose families had lived in the Shuf for generations. The Druze militia had the backing of the Syrian regime, and Syrian troops are believed to have shelled Christian areas in the Shuf in support of Druze operations. That same month, the Lebanese Forces suffered a major defeat in West Beirut while fighting against Druze and Shi'i militiamen. The Shi'i militias, supported by the Druze, moved against Lebanese army units in the area to avenge an army artillery attack on their positions. They drove the Lebanese Forces from West Beirut as well. The ejection of the Lebanese Forces and the Lebanese army from West Beirut was a major blow to the Gemayel government's credibility. It meant that Amin and his colleagues had lost control of half of the Lebanese capital.

It was also in February 1984 that the U.S. government decided to withdraw its troops from Lebanon. International criticism of the U.S. role there had been mounting for several months. On February 6, Italian president Sandro Pertini, whose peacekeeping force in Lebanon had stuck to keeping the peace and protecting civilians, thereby earning the respect and gratitude of thousands of Palestinians, declared in a radio broadcast that "American Marines have become hostage to Israeli policy. . . . Let us speak plainly, the Americans are remaining in Lebanon only to defend Israel, not peace." Four days later, without informing Amin Gemayel of his decision, President Reagan ordered the marines to withdraw.

The departure of the Americans left Amin in a weaker position than ever. His situation was rendered even more precarious by the recent disintegration of the Lebanese army. It had fallen apart at the end of 1983 when Nabih Beri called on Shi'is serving with the army to disobey orders. Subsequently, entire units of the 30,000-strong U.S.-trained and -equipped army deserted. The troops returned to their respective sectarian communities.

In March 1984, under pressure from the Syrians and from opposition groups inside Lebanon, Amin decided to annul the May 17, 1983, accord with Israel. The following month, he put together a new, Syrian-approved cabinet, known as the National Unity Cabinet, which included Nabih Beri and Walid Jumblatt, Kamal's son, who headed the PSP. Amin's about-face delighted many of his opponents, but it also caused serious divisions within the Maronite community. Moreover, it was at this point that Amin suddenly found himself deprived of the one man whose influence with the Maronites had always been of immense assistance to him — his father. Pierre Gemayel, who had backed his son's decision to accommodate the Syrians' demands, died of heart failure on August 30, 1984. In a eulogy broadcast by the state-controlled radio station, the announcer declared: "Lebanon has lost one of its most laudable figures while the country was still in need of him."

In March and April 1985, units of the Lebanese Forces suffered yet another significant defeat, this

Lebanese army troops play cards in a rare moment of calm along the notorious "Green Line" that separates East and West Beirut. Many non-Christian Lebanese accused Amin Gemayel of attempting to transform the army into a Maronite-dominated force.

time in the city of Sidon, situated on the coast to the southwest of the Shuf. The Lebanese Forces attempted to capitalize on the Israelis' withdrawal from the city. A Syrian-backed coalition of Druze, Sunni, and Shi'i militias drove the Lebanese Forces out of the city, triggering a mass exodus of the local Christian population.

It was now perfectly clear that the period of dominance the Maronites had enjoyed in the aftermath of the departure of the PLO had ended. With the decline of the Lebanese Forces during 1984 and 1985, Israeli influence in Lebanon had also faded, and most observers recognized that this situation offered the Syrian regime of Hafez al-Asad an opportunity for consolidation in Lebanon.

6

The Inflexible Sectarian

Those leaders within the Maronite community who opposed Gemayel's turn toward Syria took action early in 1985. In March, Samir Ja'ja', who had supervised the attack on the Franjiehs in June 1978, led a revolt against Gemayel's government. Ja'ja' had opposed the idea of a Lebanese rapprochement with Syria from the beginning. Now, at the head of what he called the Christian Decision Movement, Ja'ja' quickly gained the support of the other leaders of the Lebanese Forces. He also secured the backing of Solange Gemayel, Bashir's widow. The rebels demanded an end to all relations with Syria.

The revolt was a complete failure. Ja'ja's forces were defeated in Sidon and elsewhere. Ja'ja' himself finally realized that he had no choice but to capitulate in April, when a conference of Christian leaders responded to Syrian demands for an end to the rebellion. This coalition issued a statement declaring that Lebanon had a special relationship with Syria and that Lebanese unity had to be preserved at all costs.

In December 1985, further conflict erupted

> *The goal of the Lebanese government and people is first and foremost to purge the land of all non-Lebanese military presence.*
> —AMIN GEMAYEL

Members of the Hizb Allah Shi'i movement burn an American flag on the tarmac of the Beirut airport in June 1985. Nearby stood a TWA jet hijacked by a group of Lebanese Shi'i a few days earlier. The passengers on the jet were released only after lengthy negotiations.

In January 1985, relatives of kidnapping victims stage demonstrations along the Green Line in Beirut.

within the Maronite community. The Syrians had been sponsoring negotiations aimed at a new peace agreement among the various Lebanese communities for several months. During the negotiations, they had managed to secure the support of Eli Hubeika, who had taken over the leadership of the Lebanese Forces following the failure of Ja'ja's insurrection. On December 28, Hubeika, Beri, and Jumblatt signed a new accord.

Gemayel, backed by the other Maronite leaders, denounced the peace plan immediately. He, along with the other leaders of the Lebanese Forces and the Kataib, felt that the agreement reduced the political power of the Maronite community. They also considered the accord a virtual invitation to the Syrians to increase their domination over Lebanon. In mid-January of 1986, fighting between Hubeika's followers and other Maronite groups erupted throughout the Maronite heartland. Gemayel called out the Kataib militia to attack Hubeika's forces, and on January 15, Ja'ja', who still held a senior command with the Lebanese Forces, brought his own followers into the battle in support of Gemayel.

Hubeika and his followers were quickly defeated. Hubeika himself fled the country. For the Syrians, who had devoted a great deal of time and energy to cultivating Hubeika and his peace accord, this latest development came as a major blow both to their prestige and to their plans for Lebanon. The Syrian government now turned yet again to its allies in Lebanon, the Druze and the Shi'is. Their militiamen quickly commenced operations against Christian areas and even bombarded the presidential palace in Bikfayah.

Following a March 1985 bombing, banners bearing anti-American slogans hang from the skeletal remains of a West Beirut building. The bombing—a failed attempt to assassinate Shaykh Fadl Allah, the leader of the radical Shi'i movement, Hizb Allah—was allegedly financed by the U.S. government and overseen by CIA director William Casey.

In addition to ordering the Druze and Shi'i militias into the field, the Syrians, as part of their effort to intimidate Gemayel, resorted to other weapons. They used car bombings in Christian neighborhoods, assassination attempts on Gemayel's top aides, and the mounting of a propaganda campaign by their Lebanese proxies to bring about Gemayel's political isolation. Jumblatt had already made a notorious statement calling cooperation with Gemayel "treason," and Beri now issued a declaration in which he asserted that the president no longer represented Lebanon.

Eli Hubeika, the head of the Lebanese Forces, leaves a meeting in Damascus after signing an accord with the Shi'i and Druze militia leaders, Nabih Beri and Walid Jumblatt.

Gemayel's new policy of opposition to Syria received a positive response from the majority of Maronites, however, and to some extent engendered renewed communal unity. Gemayel and several other Maronite leaders, including Camille Chamoun, staged a series of meetings aimed at unifying Christian opposition to the Syrians and their allies. At the same time, the Kataib and the Lebanese Forces began to cooperate more closely. To many Lebanese, it began to seem as if the worst days of the 1975–76 period had returned. Fighting between Christians and Muslims now raged just as violently as it had then, and the country was once again on the verge of disintegration.

Although Gemayel survived this crisis, he continued to prove unable to solve the numerous problems he faced. Israel and Syria retained a substantial military presence in Lebanon, and both countries continued to meddle in Lebanon's internal affairs.

Members of a Lebanese Shi'i family clean the family weapons outside their home near the Green Line, in the center of the capital, in 1985. Fighting there had recently claimed a number of victims.

Fighting between the sectarian militias remained widespread, and the social and economic problems resulting from the violence became increasingly severe.

Gemayel's powers were severely limited. He had little real authority as president, and his government actually controlled only a small proportion of Lebanon. Within his own community, there were, and continue to be, powerful political and military forces that monitor his every move and do not hesitate to oppose him whenever they deem it appropriate. He failed to respond to reasonable demands for reform that emanated from the Druze, Sunni, and Shi'i communities. Following the departure of the PLO from Lebanon, he and his followers continued to treat the Palestinians as a people undeserving of even the most basic rights.

Gemayel also often failed to act as the leader of Lebanon even when he had a chance to do so. Although he often spoke of the need for reform, he

Amin Gemayel confers in Geneva with Syrian foreign minister Abdel Halim Khaddam in 1983. In May the Gemayel government had signed an agreement with Israel that was to lead to a withdrawal of Israeli troops from Lebanon.

generally intervened to prevent changes from taking place. He is a Maronite and a Gemayel, and the defense of his own community's interests remains one of his most fundamental preoccupations. Rabinovich's assessment of the view that Gemayel's main opponents took of him when he was being backed by the United States and Israel can, to some extent, be seen as indicative of Gemayel's general position: "To his Lebanese rivals — the Druzes, the Shi'is, Suleiman [Franjieh], and Rashid Karami — [Gemayel] was a [Kataib] president seeking to perpetuate his community's privileged position, working to further his family's and party's interests, and laboring to resist changes that should have come about before — and were unquestionably necessary after — the summer of 1982."

Perhaps the most creditable initiatives that Gemayel undertook between 1982 and 1985 were the two peace conferences he organized. The first was

In October 1982, Amin Gemayel visited Paris and met with French president François Mitterand. As a member of the Lebanese parliament and, later, as president, Gemayel traveled on a number of occasions to countries in the Middle East and Europe as well as to the United States.

held in Geneva, Switzerland, in November 1983, the second in Lausanne, Switzerland, in March 1984. The conferences brought together the leaders of the Maronite, Sunni, Druze, and Shi'i communities, but the spirit of compromise and willingness to consider reform that occasionally prevailed during the talks seemed to evaporate once the participants returned to Lebanon.

Gemayel also attempted to secure international support for his peace efforts. In the first years of his presidency, he frequently traveled abroad and met with a number of foreign heads of state. On October 18, 1982, in New York, he addressed both the UN Security Council and the UN General Assembly. In November 1983 he met with Pope John Paul II. He also held discussions with several Arab leaders, including al-Asad of Syria.

In early June 1987, Lebanese prime minister Rashid Karami was killed by a bomb blast. His coffin was carried through the streets of his hometown, Tripoli, before his burial. His death was yet another setback for the Gemayel government; Karami was one of the last Muslim leaders willing to serve in the cabinet.

Ultimately, however, Gemayel's diplomatic efforts yielded very little in the way of benefits for Lebanon. In the period from 1985 to mid-1987, a series of events occurred about which Gemayel found he could do nothing. In 1986, battles between al-Amal and the Palestinians became frequent and continued unchecked into 1987. Another major problem was the kidnapping of foreign nationals by Lebanese extremists. Among those who fell victim to this form of terrorism were faculty members at the American University in Beirut and Church of England emissary Terry Waite. In June 1987, Prime Minister Rashid Karami, one of the few Muslim leaders who were still willing to cooperate with Gemayel, was assassinated. In July 1987, the Druze and Shi'i militias, along with a number of Sunni militias, banded together to form an organization called the

Shi'i supporters of Nabih Beri celebrate in West Beirut after Beri was reelected head of the Shi'i al-Amal movement in 1986. Beri faced strong opposition, however, from within the Shi'i community, especially from radical factions that sought a more hardline approach to the political situation in Lebanon.

Amin Gemayel meets with journalists in Paris in July 1983. Gemayel spoke of his efforts to secure peace and unity for his beleaguered country. For many non-Maronite Lebanese, however, Gemayel's policies showed him to be a Maronite leader first and the president of Lebanon second.

Unification and Liberation Front. Its principal goals, according to the statements it issued, were Gemayel's resignation and the overthrow of his government.

Amin Gemayel's term of office will come to an end in 1988. His tenure will probably be seen in a negative light. Much of the responsibility for the violence that has wracked Lebanon for the past five years seems to lie with the Maronite community and its leading spokesmen. A few lines from Norton's essay may perhaps suffice to describe the situation in which Gemayel's own intransigence has helped to place him: "The Lebanese . . . want peace," he writes, "but each faction wants it on its own terms. Leadership struggles within the Sunni, [Shi'i], and Maronite communities are unlikely to end soon, and there will be no early halt to the intersectarian fighting that springs from irreconcilable visions of Lebanon's future. . . . While most sectarian leaders condemn partition, partition is emerging nonetheless. Lebanon is destined to be a state in fragments for years to come."

──────────Further Reading──────────

Azar, Edward E. *The Emergence of a New Lebanon: Fantasy or Reality?*. New York: Praeger, 1984.

Barakat, Halim. *Lebanon in Strife: Student Preludes to the Civil War*. Austin University of Texas Press, 1977.

Bender, David L. *Middle East: Opposing Views*. St. Paul, MN: Greenhaven, 1982.

Deeb, Marius. *Lebanese Civil War*. New York: Praeger, 1980.

Gale, Jack. *Lebanon Time-Bomb*. London: New Park Publications, 1982.

Gemayel, Amin, *Peace and Unity*. Gerrards Cross, England: Colin Smythe, 1984.

Gilmour, David. Lebanon: *The Fractured Country*. New York: St. Martin's, 1983.

Goldschmidt, Jr., Arthur. *A Concise History of the Middle East*. Boulder, CO: Westview 1979.

Gordon, David C. *The Republic of Lebanon: Nation in Jeopardy*. Boulder, CO: Westview, 1983.

Goria, Wade R. *Sovereignty and Leadership in Lebanon: 1943–1976*. London: Ithaca Press, 1985.

Hof, Frederic C. *Galilee Divided: The Israel-Lebanon Frontier 1916–1984*. Boulder, CO: Westview, 1985.

Khalidi, Walid. *Conflict and Violence in Lebanon: Confrontation in the Middle East*. Cambridge, MA: Harvard Studies in International Affairs, 1979.

Laqueur, Walter, and Barry Rubin. *The Israel-Arab Reader*. New York: Penguin, 1975.

Newman, Gerald. *Lebanon*. New York: Franklin Watts, 1978.

Randal, Jonathan C. *The Tragedy of Lebanon: Christian Warlords, Israeli Adventurers, and the War in Lebanon*. London: Chatto and Windus, 1983.

Salibi, Kamal S. *Crossroads to Civil War: Lebanon 1958–1976*. Delmar, NY: Caravan Books, 1976.

Shaked, Haim, and Itamar Rabinovich *Middle East & the United States: Images, Perceptions, & Policies*. Brunswick, NJ: Transaction, 1980.

Sobel, Lester A., ed. *Palestinian Impasse: Arab Guerrillas & International Terror*. New York: Facts on File, 1977.

Chronology

Nov. 6, 1905	Pierre Gemayel born
1920	League of Nations mandate proclaims France as governing power over Syria and Lebanon
Sept. 1, 1920	France establishes Greater Lebanon
May 23, 1926	Lebanese Constitution enacted
1936	Pierre Gemayel participates in Summer Olympic Games in Berlin
Nov. 1936	Founds the Kataib Party
Jan. 22, 1942	Amin Gemayel born in Bikfayah, Lebanon
1943	National Pact created, urging cooperation between Maronites and Sunnis
Nov. 22, 1943	Lebanon gains independence
Nov. 10, 1947	Bashir Gemayel born
May 13, 1948	The nation of Israel created
1958	National crisis emerges in Lebanon between pro-Western and anti-Western factions
Oct. 1958	Crisis ends; Pierre Gemayel appointed to new cabinet
Aug. 1960	Wins parliament seat
Aug. 1964	Loses presidential election
June 1967	Arab armies badly defeated by Israel in Six-Day War
Aug. 30, 1967	Triple Alliance formed
Nov. 1969	PLO and Lebanese government sign Cairo Agreement
March 20, 1970	Bashir Gemayel and militiamen attack Palestinian convoy
Aug. 1970	Pierre Gemayel again defeated in presidential election
Dec. 1970	Amin Gemayel elected to Parliament
April 1973	Israeli agents assassinate three Palestinians in Beirut
April 13, 1975	Kataib militiamen fire on busload of Palestinians, starting Lebanese civil war
March 1976	Syrian army enters Lebanon
July 1976	Bashir Gemayel appointed commander of the Kataib militia
Aug. 1976	Elected commander of Lebanese forces
Aug. 12, 1976	Fall of Tel al-Za'tar camp
March 1978 and June 1982	Israel invades Lebanon
Aug. 23, 1982	Bashir Gemayel elected president of Lebanon
Sept. 14, 1982	Assassinated in Beirut
Sept. 16, 1982	Massacres at Sabra and Shatila camps
Sept. 21, 1982	Amin Gemayel elected president of Lebanon
Aug. 29, 1984	Pierre Gemayel dies of a heart attack

Index

Matthew S. Gordon was born in Princeton, New Jersey, and grew up in Lebanon, where his parents taught at the American University in Beirut. He received his B.A. in history from Drew University in 1979 and is currently enrolled in the graduate program for Middle East studies at Columbia University. He expects to receive his doctorate in 1989. He is the author of *Khomeini* in the Chelsea House series WORLD LEADERS —PAST & PRESENT.

Arthur M. Schlesinger, jr., taught history at Harvard for many years and is currently Albert Schweitzer Professor of the Humanities at City University of New York. He is the author of numerous highly praised works in American history and has twice been awarded the Pulitzer Prize. He served in the White House as special assistant to Presidents Kennedy and Johnson.